SOLO RETIREMENT

SOLO RETIREMENT

How to Make the Prime of Your Life the Time of Your Life

JUDY SALWEN

DODD, MEAD & COMPANY, NEW YORK

Copyright © 1983 by Judy Salwen
All rights reserved
No part of this book may be reproduced in any form
without permission in writing from the publisher
Printed in the United States of America

1 2 3 4 5 6 7 8 9 10

Library of Congress Cataloging in Publication Data

Salwen, Judy.
　Solo retirement.

　1. Retirement—United States.　2. Single people—
United States.　3. Middle age—United States.　I. Title.
HQ1064.U5S25　1983　　646.7′9　　83-8909
ISBN 0-396-08151-7

*To my wonderful children,
Andrea, Valerie and Kevin,
Whose love reassured me
That, while solo, I am not alone*

Contents

ACKNOWLEDGMENTS	ix
INTRODUCTION	xi
1. FINANCIAL FOCUS	1
2. WHERE TO LIVE	25
3. YOUR HEALTH	69
4. LEISURE FOR A LIFETIME	98
5. SOLO TRAVELING	116
6. WORK IS JUST A FOUR-LETTER WORD	140
7. LEGAL LOOKOUTS	165
8. PUTTING IT ALL TOGETHER	197

Acknowledgments

My sincere thanks to Douglas Horn, of Douglas Horn & Co., CPAs, Valley Stream, New York, who helped plant the seed; Sid Friedman, Director, News Operations, NBC Radio News, who helped nurture it; John J. Younker, investment counselor with the New York City firm of L. F. Rothschild, Unterberg, Towbin, for his help with the financial chapter; and, to Margaret Norton, senior editor with Dodd, Mead & Company, for her expert professional guidance.

Introduction

A marked change has been taking place in American demographics over the past decade or two. It results from a number of trends: a diminution in family size (deriving in part from world population concerns, in part from the advent and acceptance of effective contraceptive techniques); a lifting of the stigma associated with separation and divorce; the new acceptability of the singles life-style; increased life expectancy; the movement of more and more women, both single and married, into the workplace. The median duration of marriages in the United States, for example, has dropped to six and a half years—the seven-year itch has become the six-and-one-half-year sign-off. In 1940, 1.2 percent of Americans were divorced; by the late 1970s, that figure had quadrupled to 4.8 percent—almost one in twenty. During the same time, the proportion of those never married has risen just as steadily. And the trend continues.

According to the 1981 *Statistical Abstract of the United States,* 8,840,000 of the 44,504,000 Americans in the preretirement age group (ages forty-five to sixty-four)—almost one in five, that is—are either widowed or divorced or have never been married. (For women in the fifty-five to sixty-four age group, the figure is 38 percent.) Of the 15,098,000 aged sixty-five to seventy-four in 1981, 5,470,000 were without a spouse—over 36 percent. The 14.3 million single Americans in these two age groups are the people I had in mind when writing this book.

As a preretirement specialist, I often address audiences on the need to plan in midlife for the retirement years ahead. I cover issues pertaining to leisure, housing, careers, finances, health, and legal matters.

Recently, while appearing before a business audience, I noticed blank looks on some faces each time I said, "Speak to your spouse about. . . ." I was puzzled by this reaction. Then it dawned on me that some members of the audience were like me, single—either widowed, divorced, separated, or simply never married. Today whenever I speak to groups, I immediately inquire about the composition of the audience. Determining the proportion of singles and couples in the audience helps me communicate more effectively. I now recommend that, where possible, corporations engaging my services hold separate sessions for singles and couples. That way I can concentrate on the different needs peculiar to either situation. I can spend time on points of concern that specifically relate to listeners' single or married status. The middle-aged world is no longer one of couples only.

A further awakening occurred when I discovered there was little resource material addressing the needs of midlife singles. Books dealing with planning for retirement are typically directed at couples and usually

INTRODUCTION

assume there are (adult) children on the scene. The existence of close family ties is implicit, as is the assumption that the prospective retiree is male. It is to fill the resultant information gap that I've written this book. It's time someone addressed the situation of planning for solo retirement, by people of either sex. It is a situation with special problems and challenges, but, on the other hand, one that offers broad opportunities for freedom—in terms of movement, possible range of activity, and general life-style.

Most singles are comfortable with the word *midlife*, but when they hear *retire*, many of them bristle. Some firmly declare they will always work, not realizing the meaning of *retirement* itself has changed. Sooner or later everyone retires, if only through the process of aging. For some, retirement may include staying on the job well past the traditional age of sixty-five (or the legal age of seventy for some occupations), perhaps with an altered work schedule permitting more free time. To others it may mean opting for early retirement from a regular job at fifty-five or sixty, with still vigorous years ahead to devote to travel or leisure pursuits. At any age, it may mean a long-desired opportunity to pull up stakes—to relocate geographically, to reorder priorities, to reassess oneself in terms of personal choices for the ten, twenty, thirty, or more years remaining.

The choices can be bewildering. For some singles contemplating retirement, a major upheaval, both mental and physical, is in store. For others the transition is easy. Sound preretirement planning that considers the full spectrum of life issues, financial, social, and occupational, together with all the ramifications these involve—always eases the transition. Indeed, it can open new worlds. To be most effective, this planning must be sensitive to the special emotional needs of the single person at midlife or older. These needs concern the threat of loneliness, an absence of family bonds, and the necessity of making decisions alone.

Many people wait too late to make retirement plans. Retirement often seems a distant eventuality. Some confuse retirement with preparing for the end and therefore choose to avoid the important issues now. They forfeit certain advantages of time. At forty it is difficult to think of yourself retiring. And yet the time to set certain financial wheels in motion or to lay the groundwork for an eventual retirement home (particularly if you are seeking a less expensive, not yet "developed" area) is in your forties. At fifty or sixty, the thought of retirement generally becomes more acceptable, more of a reality. People start thinking about retirement. They begin to make plans. They attend retirement programs, and they ask questions such as those raised by my audiences. In fact, in the lectures, workshops, seminars, and counseling sessions I regularly conduct in different parts of the country, questions come pouring forth. These questions, sometimes voiced as statements, express the gut concerns of those now contemplating retirement. Many are repeated over and over. In this book I've gathered those that singles regularly ask me, framing them into a dialogue covering the indicated subject areas. The material given here has been designed to help you analyze personal goals,

INTRODUCTION

take stock of the resources you have, and determine the best approach for you. It is not intended as a rigid catechism. Approach the information here with your situation in mind. Adjust and readjust your own answers to the questions presented according to your needs and circumstances and how they change.

While this book is directed to the single person who is still employed, nothing prevents those already retired from adapting the material here to their needs. For the reader under forty-five, this book has purpose, too. Not only will it aid in identifying what planning ahead you could do while time is still very much on your side, but it can make you aware of the needs of singles close to you, helping you to provide significant support to people living alone whom you care about.

As you the midlife single go into this important quarter of your life, consider the information here against your background of experience and your sense of purpose and direction. You will be well on your way to a successful retirement. Let us begin on an immediate positive note by discarding the concept that *alone* means lonely. Retirement can be as much a beginning as an end. Learn to view the decades ahead as fully creative years, richly rewarding, free, and fun-filled. Make the prime of your life the time of your life!

SOLO RETIREMENT

1
Financial Focus

Here and Now Equals Plus and Minus

I'm really worried about finances. In these uncertain times, balancing the budget becomes more and more difficult. I'll probably retire alone, but I'm not sure I can manage my finances alone. Do I really have to?

Maybe you'll be retiring alone, but financial help and information are more abundant than ever. For assistance with your financial situation and to help you plan ahead, you can look to family service agencies, county extension services, fraternal organizations, trade unions, senior citizen centers, libraries, adult education centers, and community colleges. Many companies also offer preretirement advice in group or individual counseling sessions in which participants gain familiarity with pension, Social Security, and Medicare benefits. By turning to any of these readily available sources when you need them, you'll have help managing your finances even though you live alone.

But even so, no matter how many advisers or professional opinions I get, in the long run I will have to manage my finances myself, won't I?

Perhaps that can be an asset. Who can serve you better? Unless you are in a position to engage someone to supervise your finances, a financial management service, for example, you will have to make the ultimate decisions.

Teach yourself to make those decisions in a knowledgeable way. Confer with professionals, with valued friends, and with the groups cited above. Use your middle years to read about maintaining solvency in retirement. Start planning now. There are many books available, simple and sophisticated, to suit different incomes and life-styles. Find the appropriate one for you.

Think about joining a self-help group. Financially oriented groups are sponsored by banks, brokerage houses, singles' organizations, and education centers.

Most important, work toward becoming one of the numerous middle-aged singles who find handling finances enjoyable. The challenge of being in charge can be gratifying. You won't become an expert overnight, but with study, time, and practice you can become financially able. You can establish yourself in a secure position. So use those middle years to your own financial advantage.

Sometimes I think I'd like that better than using some of the financial professionals around. There's no end to the mail from people and organizations clamoring to do the right thing for me. How does the single person pick and choose financial advisers?

It is true that the quantity of financial advisers is enormous. Accountants, investment counselors, bankers, stockbrokers, and insurance agents are only some of the financial specialists eager to help. Some advisers earn their living that way; others extend themselves because it is part of their job.

Some singles choose to seek the advice of several specialists. From their viewpoint, multiple counsel is valuable because it offers useful information from a diversity of perspectives.

If you can afford to pay consultation fees, engage a specialist. If you can't, seek free advice—there's a lot of good advice available at no charge. Before you select financial advisers, ask yourself these practical questions: Are the advisers recommended by successful friends? Which ones are recognized by associations or reputable business enterprises? What credentials does each adviser hold? Whose personality pleases you most? Look for advisers who understand and respect your life-style and thus will counsel you accordingly. Compose a list of the qualities most important to you in people who will advise you. Qualities such as knowledge, reliability, and caring are essential. Then go with the best available, affordable person or persons. Fortunately, qualified financial advisers are abundant.

The Years Ahead: How Much?

There is so much to learn and only me to learn it. I know where my finances are now. How much comes in and how much goes out while I am working is no mystery. But how can I learn about managing retirement finances? Where do I begin?

Begin now, in your middle years. Do your planning. Set your goals. Then take appropriate steps. First estimate what your income will be when you retire. Where will your income stem from? Will you have income from part-time work, from Social Security, from an I.R.A. account, pensions, annuities, interest, dividends, real estate, veterans' benefits, and disability payments? Estimate your expenses in retirement. (Use the chart at the end of this chapter to help you.) Keep in mind that the average person needs 60 to 80 percent of preretirement income to maintain the same standard of living in retirement.

That's a start. Where do I go from there?

Set your wheels in motion during the work years. Consult services that give free or inexpensive information and provide resource aids that deal with retirement finances. Banks issue literature about money basics in retirement. They often offer other valuable aid. I know of a bank that has set up a women's exchange center to alert women to investment opportunities and to assist them in financial management. This has proved very useful to at least one recently divorced woman.

Try to accumulate as substantial an investment fund as possible between now and retirement. Investment income, or unearned income as it is commonly termed, does not reduce Social Security benefits as do earnings from wages and salary. Be certain to keep abreast of changes in Social Security. Send for the free booklets issued on Social Security benefits—your local Social Security Office will have them. If your income bracket warrants it, shelter from taxes as much current income as possible. Remember an I.R.A. account is a shelter for taxes during your working years. Look into rental property, United States savings bonds, owning a house, mutual funds invested on tax-exempt securities, and municipal bonds.

What if my income does not warrant such investments?
Then plan ways to invest whatever surplus or extras you have so that your money makes as much money as possible for you. For example, an I.R.A. (Individual Retirement Account) is a practical investment for this purpose. That way, income from investments made now builds retirement income. Put your money to work carefully and intelligently.

Expecting the Unexpected

Okay, that's advice for building retirement income. What about emergencies? Isn't that something the single person must make financial plans for?
Let us start from scratch and look at it this way. The older you are and the less money you have, the more you should stress safety and income to meet current needs. Everyone needs savings for emergencies, guaranteed income to meet expenses, and investment income to keep ahead of inflation. Therefore, in addition to a realistic budget, a sound investment program and estate planning, the middle-aged single should be concerned with sufficient insurance coverage to meet

emergencies. You should plan for possible emergencies and disability before retirement.

All right, but where's the money and care to come from if I am faced with a long-term convalescence?

Adequate insurance coverage is the best answer to this problem. If disability strikes, you may be at a disadvantage being alone, because long-term convalescent care can be costly. You may need help with housekeeping, shopping, nursing, and other kinds of care. That requires much money in today's economy. The right combination of income-supplementing disability and major medical coverage is essential to meet these emergency expenses.

Speak with an insurance friend about maintaining a comprehensive, noncancelable insurance program that will provide protection in the event of long-term disability. The plan is to replace lost wages and to meet convalescent costs without liquidating investment assets. But be aware that the age factor may increase the cost of such coverage if you wish to take it out in your late years.

Speaking of insurance, would you recommend life insurance coverage for middle-aged singles?

Obviously there is little need for life insurance if you have no immediate dependents. So reallocate those dollars elsewhere. If you have a life insurance policy from the past and the need for this type of insurance has diminished, examine the conversion privileges in your policy. Explore various options available to you by consulting with a financial adviser and your insurance agent. Then make an educated decision.

There are so many things on my mind, and I'm not happy thinking of ill health or disability.
　Who is? That's why it is so important to plan ahead and protect yourself by making the right choices in insurance. Also keep in mind that medical and disability insurance are simply two types of insurance available. Income can be produced through as well as spent on insurance. Don, a bachelor, found that considerable equity could be built up in whole life insurance. He chose to borrow against that equity at very attractive interest rates and then invested this money in higher-paying investments. Herb, a widower, owned a life insurance policy from his army days. He decided to cash that policy in and convert to another with a paid-up status. This covered him for life to the amount of the face value of the new policy. Harriet, a widow, selected the option of converting to an extended-term status, covering herself for the full face amount but for less than her full lifetime. The idea is to locate an insurance agent you can trust to examine your particular situation and advise you appropriately. It is also sensible to consult your financial adviser for an objective opinion on the best way to organize your insurance arrangements.

Would you say Social Security is another type of insurance? I'm counting on Social Security income when I retire.

Right now figure on Social Security as it exists for the single today, and do what you can at the same time to build retirement income from other sources. As things now stand, for example, a divorcee is entitled to Social Security benefits when her ex-husband starts collecting retirement or disability payments provided she is sixty-two or older and was married to him at least ten years. A widow who remarried at sixty or older can continue receiving Social Security income without any reduction in the amount. For widows fifty and older who become disabled, Medicare may be available after receiving twenty-four consecutive disability checks. (For other stipulations on Medicare and disability, consult your local Social Security office.)

At the same time, if you are in your middle years, take advantage of the provisions of the 1981 Economic Recovery Tax Act. If you have extra funds, open a private pension fund by investing in an Individual Retirement Account or in a Keogh plan account. Even if you are enrolled in a company or union pension plan, this act entitles you to open your own pension fund, providing you distinct tax advantages.

Are there any other kinds of insurance the single person should be aware of?

You are your own insurance. Think in terms of building a new career to supplement retirement income. Find out what Social Security regulations are regarding the maximum earnings allowed in retirement. (We'll talk more about possible work opportunities in a later chapter.)

Investing in a Single Future

What sort of investment program works best for singles?

Since there is usually only you to support, look into an investment program that provides small risks and suitable income. You don't have to take as many chances as your married counterpart. Seek an investment program that distributes your investments. You might consider investing in common stocks, in preferred stocks, in government and corporate bonds, in mutual funds or the money market, in real estate, or in annuities. Be an aware single like Ted, a divorced middle-aged man, who knows precisely what his taxable income must be after deductions and exemptions. That way he keeps alert to investments that are advantageous for him as a single man.

Can you give me a better idea of what's involved?

Well, if you are in a higher tax bracket, you'll want to consider tax-exempt investments such as municipal bonds, the IOUs issued by cities and other local government units when they borrow. The interest an investor receives on such IOUs is exempt from federal income taxes, although it may be subject to state and local income taxes. Your state tax bureau will be able to tell you what the situation is in this regard where you live.

From your point of view, are there investment advantages in putting funds in an Individual Retirement Account or a Keogh pension plan?

There certainly are. One simple reason is that this do-it-yourself retirement fund allows you to make annual contributions to a nest egg. The contributions are tax deductible, and the interest earnings each year are tax-free. Taxes must ultimately be paid on earnings in the fund, but not until after retirement when your tax bracket will probably be much lower. In terms of the investment itself, check to be certain the interest you receive on your IRA or Keogh contribution is the highest obtainable. Shop around for the highest rate. Compare offerings from different banks, investment companies, and other sources. If you are getting an old interest rate that doesn't keep up with inflation, it may well pay to transfer your IRA/Keogh from one investment service to another. Again, shop around for the one that offers you the top interest rate, with minimum risk, even if you pay a penalty for withdrawal for transfer purposes. At the same time, be sure it affords you a large enough rate of interest to compensate for the dollar loss sustained as result of withdrawal and new placement. Finally, speak to your financial adviser about any changes in IRA and Keogh occasioned by the changes in the tax laws.

Good luck in becoming a knowledgeable investor!

When Planning Bears Unplanned Fruit

It is possible to become investment proficient. But one thing you can't plan for is life and death. What good does all the planning in the world do, when suddenly you are left alone? My husband and I planned our estates, and here I am today, middle-aged and alone. All the planning in the world didn't help me.

Sometimes it is difficult to make sense out of the unexpected. But let's look at where you are now, since nothing we can do can change the past. The fact that your husband and you did plan your estate probably saved you a great deal of unnecessary hardship. It certainly saved you taxes, legal fees, and state disposition of who gets what when no will is left. In addition, if you were the beneficiary of a company policy, amounts paid you were excludable from gross income. (There is a maximum amount excludable. Here again, your financial adviser or the company's representative is the person to consult.)

Be aware, too, that the executor of an estate may elect not to pay an estate tax for a certain period. That's perfectly in order, as long as interest on the tax for that period is paid each year. After this time, the estate tax liability can be paid in yearly installments over a specified number of years. Check this, too, with your financial adviser.

What all this means is planning your estate with your late husband gave you safety and structure and the time to learn how to handle your individual finances.

What should I do? I haven't made any changes in my estate planning since my husband died several years ago?

It is time to get on with individual estate planning. First, decide which professional you are going to work with on planning your estate. Next, be certain you are up-to-date in your understanding of the tax laws as they affect estate planning. The tax bite on a single person's estate can be quite heavy if the estate is at all considerable. If you own a sizeable estate, you may want to make gifts within the tax-exempt allowance to save money later on. These gifts can be made in the present. Aside from easing the tax bite to your heirs, the pleasure of giving and the joy of the recipient will be added bonuses for you.

There are other alternatives available to you. You can establish trusts. For that matter, you can choose to use up all your money while still alive. There are several ways to minimize the estate tax bite. Whatever you decide, do not undertake a do-it-yourself job in estate planning. That is hazardous. You risk substantial loss in what you leave behind. With laws undergoing frequent change, obtaining the advice of financial experts will prove a worthwhile expenditure.

I understand an estate should have executors. Whom would you advise the single person to name as executors?

This is another problem the single person faces in estate planning. Look to a trusted friend or relative, a lawyer, or, depending upon the size and complexity of your estate, the trust department of a bank to act for you in that capacity. A divorced woman, Barbara, named a cousin with sound business judgment and her brother, a successful physician, as executors. Both are caring people. When Barbara's three children reached the legal age for them to assume the role of executors, she named them to replace her cousin as one of the original choices, but left her physician brother as supervisory executor.

However you set up your estate, remember that if there is no will, the state has its own laws of intestacy determining who gets what. These laws vary in detail from state to state. The immediate family of the decedent conventionally receives first priority in distribution of the estate's assets. Close friends are accorded nothing as a rule. It is important that you have a will drawn up as quickly as possible if you haven't already done so. Otherwise, you might find your estate being distributed to distant relatives or, if you have no immediate family, going to the state.

You are speaking of large estates only, right?

The larger your estate or holdings, the more complex the planning and provisions for its disposition. That is why consultation with a financial professional is essential. However, bear in mind that everybody has an estate, whether it is a piece of furniture, a few articles of jewelry, or just the clothing on your back. If your holdings are small or minimal, planning the disposition of your possessions upon your demise can largely be done through a will. You can purchase a standard will form from a stationery or legal goods store. Fill it out and have it witnessed by another person. However, as soon as you can, have your attorney draw up a will that specifically covers your estate situation which no standard form can do as well.

If the Boat Is Rocked

What else should the person suddenly alone be sure to do?

If you find yourself alone suddenly, take immediate steps to insure your own financial safety. For example, open an individual bank account to replace a joint account you shared with your spouse. If funds are not already committed to a financial plan, request immediate payment of benefits under any insurance policy in effect for the amount of money you will need for two months.

I'm glad to have your suggestions. Everybody had advice for me when I was widowed. My head was too cluttered, and I was too distressed at that time to take intelligent financial action.

All the more reason to be sure you take care of immediate needs. Then later you can determine your net financial worth—what your assets and liabilities are, what you own and what you owe. (The difference between what you own and what you owe is your net worth.) Postpone further investment decisions until you are in control of yourself. As soon as possible, see that you have a will drawn up by a lawyer, or that your present will is brought up to date.

I'm not widowed. I'm divorced. And that was pretty sudden, too. What advice do you have for me?

Immediately open your own individual bank account and establish your own line of credit. If credit was previously granted to you solely on the basis of your ex-spouse's income, inform your creditors of your new status and establish credit under your own name. You can also establish your own line of credit by borrowing from a bank or credit union and paying back the loan on time. You can establish a credit line with department stores by opening one or more charge accounts in your own name.

Check with Social Security about benefits provisions for divorcees. Your eligibility for benefits depends upon the length of your marriage and your own employment record. If you are unemployed, find yourself a job or start preparing for a new career. When things are settled, determine your financial net worth. Leave investment decisions for later.

I'm thinking about the present. I have too little money to worry about estate planning. I'm in debt because of alimony, and I just hope my ex remarries so I'll have financial peace in retirement.

It might help to know that since 1977 eligible alimony payments are allowed as deductions from taxable gross income. As a result, singles making alimony payments can use the standard deduction rather than itemize, as previously required. Also, by keeping a personal financial statement, you can develop a debt-reduction program and see which assets are working, which are not working, and what to do. Blank statement forms are available at most banks. Think of other ways you can help yourself become solvent. Perhaps a self-help financial group for divorcees would be beneficial.

My Life-Style Is Me

I'm neither widowed nor divorced. I have always been single, and since I've always been in charge of my finances, I know how important it is to plan ahead. I don't want to be poor when I'm old.

That's the key—to use your middle years effectively and establish a solid financial foundation for retirement. Use the present to generate as much income as possible, putting surplus immediately into income-producing investments. Plot out a financial road map now for retirement later. Keep a financial statement, properly detailed and frequently updated, as a readily available reference to use in setting goals. That will provide you a current view of all your financial affairs, which makes plotting the next step easier.

What about another important financial consideration: making it possible for others to handle matters when you die?

Yes, that is very important.

Make it simple for others to handle your finances when the situation requires it. Singles should list vital papers and where they can be found. If you have a joint bank account—if you are alone and incapacitated, you may be unable to act on your own behalf—leave instructions as to where you keep your bankbook and other pertinent information. Remember: On the death of a holder of a joint bank account, the account is closed, even to the other account holder, until the estate is settled. That always takes time. If you are totally alone

FINANCIAL FOCUS 17

or old, consider appointing a conservator. Choose someone you trust, and give that person appropriate powers—*after* consultation with your attorney, who can point out fully the consequences of what you are doing. Finally, if you remarry, talk to your new spouse about investments you have made, about how to manage future investments, how to look after them, and, if possible, whom to consult when one of you dies.

Your Life Expectancy at Retirement*

Here are the latest available life expectancy figures for men and women at various ages. To give yourself a safety margin in figuring how much you will need in the years ahead, you might want to add five or six years to these official figures.

Present Age	Average Remaining Years Male	Female
50	25.0	30.9
51	24.2	30.1
52	23.4	29.2
53	22.7	28.3
54	21.9	27.5
55	21.1	26.7
56	20.4	25.8
57	19.6	25.0
58	18.9	24.2
59	18.2	23.4
60	17.5	22.6
61	16.8	21.8
62	16.2	21.0
63	15.6	20.2
64	14.9	19.5
65	14.3	18.7
66	13.7	18.0
67	13.1	17.2
68	12.6	16.5
69	12.0	15.8
70	11.5	15.1

*These figures have been provided by the National Center for Health Statistics (1979 abridged Life Table).

FINANCIAL FOCUS:
Ready money is Aladdin's lamp.
—LORD BYRON

Financial Focus

Personal Income Form I
How Much Money Will You Need in Retirement?

With this guide you can go a long way toward estimating how much money will be needed to maintain the standard of living you choose when the day comes to stop working or reduce working.

	ANNUAL INCOME Now	During Retirement
Salary	$_____	$_____
Social Security*		$_____
Pension(s)		$_____
Annuities		$_____
Interest	$_____	$_____
Dividends from savings, stocks, bonds, insurance	$_____	$_____
Real estate income	$_____	$_____
Veteran's benefits	$_____	$_____
Disability payments	$_____	$_____
Employment income	$_____	$_____
Other sources	$_____	$_____

---

*Contact the nearest Social Security office for an estimate of what you can expect to receive in Social Security benefits.

> *FINANCIAL FOCUS:*
> Annual income twenty pounds, annual expenditure nineteen nineteen six, result happiness. Annual income twenty pounds, annual expenditure twenty pounds ought and six, result misery.
> —CHARLES DICKENS

Personal Income Form II
How Much Money Will You Need in Retirement?

ANNUAL EXPENSES

	Now	During Retirement
Rent or mortgage	$_____	$_____
Home maintenance and repair	$_____	$_____
Heat and electricity	$_____	$_____
Telephone	$_____	$_____
Taxes		
Income	$_____	$_____
Property	$_____	$_____
Other	$_____	$_____
Food		
At home	$_____	$_____
Eating out	$_____	$_____
Clothing	$_____	$_____
Automobile expense		
Fuel	$_____	$_____
Repairs	$_____	$_____
Other transportation costs	$_____	$_____
Travel	$_____	$_____
Entertainment	$_____	$_____
Recreation	$_____	$_____
Insurance		
Life	$_____	$_____
Property	$_____	$_____
Other	$_____	$_____
Medical		
Doctors	$_____	$_____
Dentists	$_____	$_____
Hospitals	$_____	$_____
Medicine	$_____	$_____
Medicare	$_____	$_____
Health plans	$_____	$_____

Financial Focus

Personal gifts	$_____	$_____
Charitable gifts	$_____	$_____
Other items	$_____	$_____
	$_____	$_____
	$_____	$_____
Total	$_____	$_____

FINANCIAL FOCUS:
Money is a terrible master but an excellent servant.
—P. T. BARNUM

Financial Guideline

The older you are and/or the less money you have, the more you should stress *safety* and *income* to meet current needs. Everyone needs *savings* for emergencies; *guaranteed income* to meet expenses; *investment income* to keep ahead of inflation. Here is how three persons, ages 45, 55, and 65, might invest $20,000.

	Age 45	Age 55	Age 65
Emergency money—insured savings	$ 4,000	$ 5,000	$ 6,000
Guaranteed money—savings and corporate bonds; preferred stocks; government securities; annuities	2,000	5,000	10,000
Investment money—common stocks; investment trusts; real estate	14,000	10,000	4,000
	$20,000	$20,000	$20,000

FINANCIAL FOCUS:
Money often costs too much.
—RALPH WALDO EMERSON

Building Income

GOAL: BUILDING FINANCES FOR RETIREMENT

List ways you are building retirement income in preretirement years.

1.

2.

3.

4.

5.

6.

7.

8.

9.

10.

GOAL: ADDING TO INCOME AFTER RETIREMENT FROM THE PRESENT FULL-TIME JOB

If you are planning to add to income, list ways you will do this.

1.

2.

3.

4.

5.

6.

7.

FINANCIAL FOCUS:
Money is like a sixth sense without which you cannot make use of the other five.
—WILLIAM SOMERSET MAUGHAM

Professionals Who Can Help with Finances

Being single can mean having more time to explore and manage preretirement finances. Use this time to interview financial advisers. Select those who impress you most as knowledgeable and reliable and who understand your lifestyle.

People Who Can Advise Me Financially	I plan to visit them on:
1. My accountant	1.
2. Investment counselor	2.
3. Insurance brokers	3.
(Add your own:)	
4.	4.
5.	5.

6. _____   6. _____

7. _____   7. _____

Qualities Most Important in People Who Offer Me Financial Advice

1. _____

2. _____

3. _____

4. _____

5. _____

6. _____

FINANCIAL FOCUS:
When I was young I thought that money was the most important thing in life; now that I am old I know it is.
—OSCAR WILDE

2
Where to Live

Housing, Housing Everywhere

Let's face it. I can choose to go or not go to the movies. But when it comes to providing a suitable roof over my head for my later years, I have no choice. That has to be one of the most important decisions I have to make while I am still in my full-time work years. Don't you agree?

Be it humble or fancy, as a single retiree you should choose your retirement home with great care. This is one of the most important decisions you will make both financially and emotionally. Whether the decision is to stay put or to move, base it on an understanding of what will give you the most comfort, pleasure, convenience, security, and manageability, now and in the years to come. That is of utmost importance. Not only should your choice reflect your life-style and taste, it should provide you with a sense of neighborliness and belonging, give you some feeling of family that many singles otherwise find lacking. Planning retirement housing while you are still in the work years and taking appropriate steps necessary to realizing your choice could result in a happier retirement. The chart at the end of this chapter, "Determining Retirement Housing," should help you unscramble housing priorities.

I can use all the help available. Couples have each other to confer with when discussing where they will live in retirement. I have no one to plan this with, and I have no idea what is available.

There are several types of housing to choose from: a single-family, two-family, or multiple-family house; a rental apartment; a condominium; a cooperative apartment; group living quarters; a retirement village; a mobile home; a leisure vehicle; even a houseboat. The possibilities are numerous. You can be creative. Paul, a divorcé and an amateur craftsman, converted a barn into an attractive home. He did much of the work himself and hired contractors only to do the more technical jobs, like plumbing and heating.

Whatever your choice, be certain it provides for total living. Take into account your needs for adequate shopping, entertainment, parks, religious worship, security. Check out opportunities for cultural, educational, and recreational fulfillment. Since housing may be the major retirement expense you encounter—some singles spend as much as one-third of retirement income on housing—be certain you explore your options adequately while still in your middle years. It will assure you spend your housing dollars on what truly suits you.

How do I do that? Where do I start finding out what is available?

Start first by utilizing people resources. Discuss housing options with friends and relatives who have made informed choices. Explore what is available with professional real estate people. Refer also to retirement counselors and financial advisers—the latter will provide you much practical insight into what income will be available in retirement for housing. If you attended college, write to your college alumni office for a list of alumni who live in areas you are considering. This can give you helpful information and perhaps help you get your social life started as well, should you decide to relocate where they live.

When you have exhausted your people resources, proceed to "nonpeople" resources.

What are nonpeople resources?

These include printed materials put out by organizations and businesses. For example, a newspaper real estate section can inform you where to contact realtors and builders where there are retirement communities. Magazines, catering to mature readers, often advertise housing developments for adults near or in retirement. Check your library for books about retirement housing.

Once you pinpoint the area in which you think you would like to live, write to the local visitor's bureau—most communities of any size have such an organization—for information about points of interest, city history, ethnic neighborhoods, restaurants, and shopping. That will tune you into the pulse of the community, as will subscribing to the local newspaper for six months, to familiarize yourself with news of the area and with advertisements that will give you answers to questions like: How much does food cost? Is the area plagued with crime? What are the usual weather conditions? What cultural and recreational facilities are available? You can order telephone books from the local telephone business office. From the Yellow Pages you could learn about the goods and services obtainable in your new neighborhood.

Another suggestion is to write to the chamber of commerce in the area that interests you for free brochures and specific information on services, taxes, transportation, and real estate. If possible, visit or vacation in the area you are considering two or three times before moving there. This will allow you to gain a feeling for the area beyond what any printed word can supply.

In all your information gathering, ask about services specifically for singles that the area affords.

Would you agree that individuals are the best and most important information resources available?

Yes. This was particularly apparent in the experience of an aware friend, Celia, who discovered an innovative housing service while at a singles' fair in New York City. A booth announcing home services caught her eye, and Celia, burdened with maintenance problems since her husband died and her grown children moved away, was delighted with the exhibitor's literature. Two enterprising women had set up a singles' home service exchange, a registry of individuals interested in exchanging skills and services needed for home maintenance and survival. Their literature invited singles to become registered members for an initial six-month period. They charged a modest fee to cover a monthly mailing listing new members and people with special skills. The group she discovered is The Singles' Home Services Exchange, serving New York City, northern New Jersey, and Long Island. (Their mailing address is P.O. Box 58, Sea Cliff, New York 11579.)

Be alert to similar organizations in your area. They may be listed in the real estate section of your newspaper. If they are, great. If not, be resourceful and start such a group in your area.

Speaking of resourcefulness, I recently learned of time shares as an option in vacation housing. Many of my single friends are buying time shares in different types of price ranges.

Many people, looking for alternatives to buying or renting vacation housing, are investing in time shares. This can be an especially attractive option for retirees living on limited budgets. Buying a share in an apartment, say for one or two weeks, would include a onetime cost—usually an annual maintenance fee that includes insurance and taxes. The time share is then reserved for you during the same week or weeks every year. You can do what you like with the time—lend it, lease it, sell it, will it, or even trade it for time at other resorts through an international exchange network. Send for *The Buyer's Guide to Resort Timesharing* from the CHB Company, Box 184, Los Altos, California 94022. It is available for a small fee. Or write for free directories from Resorts Condominiums International, Box 80229, Indianapolis, Indiana 46240. You will find out how to arrange housing for enjoyable vacation time in various locations. That could be fun!

But How Do You Feel?

I am planning to stay put. I am comfortable where I live. It is familiar. It meets my emotional and psychological needs, and it is kind to my pocketbook. My late husband and I made a good home here together. We raised our family here. I have no interest in changing.

One of the reasons people remain in a present dwelling is the proximity of family and friends. This satisfies the need for personal closeness, which is particularly important to people living alone. The knowledge of local shops is another reason some people stay put. Knowing the tradespeople and existing service facilities makes life easier for some men and women. Familiarity breeds comfort. An established relationship with medical professionals is another reason people choose to remain where they are. The fact that trusted doctors and dentists are nearby provides a secure and comfortable feeling for people, particularly as they grow older. It is when all these needs are no longer satisfied that people start to think of changes.

The neighborhood I am living in is changing. I am afraid to come home late at night alone. Car service is expensive. So is taxi fare or keeping a car of my own.

When conditions change, you may have to make a housing change, too. Otherwise feelings of stress, frustration, anxiety, and fear replace former healthier feelings of pleasure, ease, and fun. If you are unsure about your situation, drawing up a two-part list could be useful. On one side, list reasons for staying where you are.

On the other side itemize reasons for moving. Which list takes more of your day-to-day needs into account?

Train yourself to become alert to changes in your surroundings. Neighborhoods do not change overnight. You will notice slight changes, compounded by additional changes, and then still more differences. When is it time to move on? That is a personal decision. But by staying aware you prepare yourself to move when necessary. You will utilize time more effectively, for one thing. You can explore housing options in advance of need. In addition, you prepare yourself psychologically because you permit yourself to accept change. Then, if you must redirect housing dollars, you will have done the groundwork and be able to resettle with a clearer sense of improving your situation.

Isn't that an oversimplification? Are facts the only considerations? How about my feeling that relocating where I know no one is upsetting?

Certainly these are feelings to take into account. But don't let them complicate things for you unnecessarily. Compounding matters by overemphasizing negative feelings when a change has to be made will just make matters more difficult for you. Of course, it is difficult to leave the familiar. After all, you know so much about where you live now. You have no guarantee of what life will be like where you are moving to. No matter how much research you engage in prior to a move, there is always some element of doubt.

But think positively. Be patient. Give yourself time to adjust, to become comfortable in your new environment. That is no easy task, but if you must relocate because your old neighborhood has changed, or if now you feel isolated because your friends have moved, fighting yourself is self-defeating. Make up your mind to do what is best for you and then get on with it. Other middle-aged and retired people do it every day. You will have access to other people; you can develop feelings of belonging. You can enjoy a sense of well-being as you feel more secure.

Select a housing situation that provides opportunities for social contacts and meaningful relationships. This is what Gloria, a middle-aged divorcee, did when the neighborhood she lived in changed. By moving to an adult housing development where people were her age, that provided a planned social program and recreation areas encouraging sociability—community swimming pool, clubhouse, tennis courts, and a nearby golf course—Gloria made a happy change and a successful adjustment.

I am not a groupie. I enjoy doing things alone. However, I must live where I have ready access to a diversity of cultural and recreational activities. That way I have much to choose from.

Whether you are a person who enjoys doing things solo or someone who enjoys the companionship of others in social, recreational, or cultural activities, accessibility is a real plus. Some people choose housing where social activities are "built in" so they do not have to go to exhausting lengths to satisfy their social needs. Barbara, who has been single all her life and enjoys doing things alone, decided to move from the suburbs smack into the heart of Manhattan. She did this in the last few years of her full-time work life. Now that she is retired, everything is convenient, often within walking distance of her apartment. Yes, she compromised, trading space for accessibility. Her city apartment is smaller, but she can easily walk to museums, movies, theaters, restaurants, and shops. There is value in having the courage to change!

I think a housing change would help me to clear up some of the internal debris that divorce has created, to put the past in perspective.

Memories are potent, particularly memories of long years with husbands and wives. That is why many people, divorced and widowed, choose to put a lid on the past and start a new life. They do this in different ways and it affects their housing situation differently, too.

Ann, a widow, still lives in the apartment she shared with her late husband. She has made her peace with the past without feeling it necessary to move.

Irving, a widower, had to move from the apartment he had shared with his late wife before he could share a life with another woman.

Nora, a divorcee, feels strongly that selling the house in which her former husband and she spent twenty-three years together was vital to her psychological recovery and the acceptance of a single life. She feels she can move ahead now into a happy life. She is no longer faced with constant reminders of an unhappy past.

A new start in a new home can do much to heal grief and replace it with pleasure. It can open you up as well to a feeling of embarking on a good future.

I would welcome a move to another location, preferably to one with a warmer climate. But the thought of my children and grandchildren living more than a thousand miles away makes me unhappy. What would be the point of moving if I could not enjoy it?

The distance from people you feel close to is an important consideration in determining where you will live. Moving can be emotionally expensive as well as financially expensive. Adjustment can involve saying good-bye to people you love, even though this jet age provides means for staying in touch. There is loss and emptiness to contend with.

Sonia, a widow, learned this at great expense. She spent a great deal of money and time flying from Florida, where she had relocated, to Boston, where her children and grandchildren lived. She missed them so much that it interfered with her adjustment to her new environment.

Weigh the pros and cons carefully. Consider these questions: How well do you adjust to new situations and to new environments? How important is it for you to be surrounded by familiar things? If you do not adjust easily, is there some way to help yourself break with the past if you decide to move?

If I decide to move, I want the right to have my grandchildren stay with me for as long as I wish. Is it true that some adult communities will not permit young children to live on the premises for extended periods?

There are developments that have such regulations, and they enforce those, too. Therefore, inquire carefully and read the small print in any contract or lease before you sign. Know exactly what you're getting into.

Apartments for Rent

I have been a homemaker most of my married life. Now that I am alone and my grown children live some distance away, I am considering selling my house and renting an apartment. What are the advantages and disadvantages of apartment living?

Renting an apartment has several advantages over homeowning. There is the freedom to move about as you please, to relocate without having to worry about disposing of real property. You can travel without having house cares to weigh you down. You are not tied down by maintenance responsibilities, such as lawns to mow, snow to shovel, the need for an exterior paint job or a furnace that needs servicing. Insurance costs are usually lower for the apartment dweller.

On the other hand, some apartment dwellers complain of feeling crowded. This can be a difficult readjustment if you are used to living in a house. It was something Carl, a widower who loves collecting and reading books, complained of. He had to sort through and compress the furniture and book collection from his ten-room house to fit into a one-bedroom apartment. Noise is another disadvantage of apartment rental. Sometimes a neighbor has a party going until the wee hours of the morning or is watching the late TV show, and those paper-thin apartment walls do not shut out sounds. Another disadvantage in renting rather than owning is that there is no build-up of equity, which could otherwise provide handy cash in your retirement years.

Whether you decide to rent an apartment or stay in your home, the important thing is to make it a well-considered decision. Take the time to review your circumstances from all angles. Careful consideration can result in a delightful residence choice for your middle and retirement years. A hasty decision can result in much unhappiness and the need to rectify a situation you experience as a mistake. That can be both financially and emotionally draining, occasioning much stress and costing hard-earned dollars. In the time available before retirement, use your investigative skills to come to informed decisions. Establish your priorities, weighed against availability of housing options, climate, location of your family, social and employment opportunities, and anything else fundamental to your needs. Then consider the pros and cons of apartment rental as compared to ownership and determine which suits you the best.

I want to fill my widowed life with more pleasure. My children are grown, and they agree that this is my time. They want me to sell the house and move into a convenient apartment. They say they will never live with me, but when they come to visit, I want them to be able to stay over. With my house, there's room. But if I were to rent a comparable apartment, it would cost me four times what I pay now, since the mortgage I have on the house is paid up.

This is where flexibility pays off. Furniture arrangements can sometimes stretch living space and thus provide extra room. To pay additional rent for rooms rarely used is poor budgetary planning. Ingenuity and good design can provide additional living space with a convertible couch or sleeper chairs for once-in-a-while overnight guests. Saying "welcome" does not have to tax the pocketbook.

Here's one more problem. I've been told not to sell my house before I'm fifty-five. But I want to move now to an apartment in the heart of the city, where as a divorced woman, I will be able to take advantage of the easy access to the theater, restaurants, art galleries—all the things I love. What's that all about?

It's about saving money on capital gains taxes, which can be considerable where real property is involved.

Pamela, a divorcee, was told she would not have to worry about any capital gains tax if she waited to sell her house until she reached age fifty-five. If she sold her house at a profit and then bought a more expensive replacement residence within eighteen months, she would not have to pay a capital gains tax even though she was younger than fifty-five. But if her new residence costs her less than the sales price of her former house, she would be responsible for a hefty capital gains tax.

The capital gains tax exemption on home sales at age fifty-five is a one-time tax privilege. Pamela's accountant advised her to wait. So did others who counseled her in financial affairs. But friends Pamela consulted advised her to sell so that she could proceed with reconstructing her life. Her grown children also encouraged her to sell before her fifty-fifth birthday, still years away. They wanted their mother to live where she would be most happy.

Pamela's decision, arrived at after serious consideration, was that financial gains, while a valuable contribution to freedom and independence, would not make up for years spent in living in a place that no longer satisfied her present needs. She sold her house before her fifty-fifth birthday, moved to a centrally located apartment, and accepted responsibility for the capital gains tax. She does not regret her decision, which cost her dollars but paid her back in joyous living.

Now that I am widowed and my friends have moved from the neighborhood, I find myself more and more alone. I am one to bask in the companionship of good friends and neighbors. People tell me to change apartments, to move to a complex where there are people my age.

The appeal of an all-adult housing complex lies in being around people your own age. Opportunities to make new friends are practically built in there, since socializing is on everybody's mind, particularly those who hover around the clubhouse, the tennis courts, or the poolside. Of course, it is not necessary to move to an all-adult complex to make new friends. If you are outgoing, an apartment complex catering to all ages—to marrieds and singles, to families with or without children—can as readily be a source of new friendships.

After his divorce, Isadore moved north from Georgia on a company assignment. He is amazed at the meaningful friends he has made with others who live in his apartment complex. First he met Louise, a divorcee, who moved into the building a month after he did and who relates easily to people. After several chance encounters in the elevator, they decided to meet for coffee together. While Louise is almost ten years Isadore's senior, they have become good friends as well as being neighbors and enjoy dinner, walks in the neighborhood, and parties together from time to time. They have enriched each other's lives. It is apparent from their situation that tales of a cold and lonely existence in the big city are not the whole story when it comes to considering life there.

Co-ops and Condos

I hear so much about condos and co-ops. What's the difference between them?

Condominiums and cooperatives are both forms of common ownership. They differ in what exactly is owned.

When you buy a condominium, you buy real estate and you receive a deed for your apartment or house, which is one unit in a multiple-unit complex. You pay property taxes directly to your local government. The complex as a whole is actually owned by the condominium owners' association. You are a voting member of the organization, and you pay a proportionate share of the cost of operating and maintaining the complex property.

When you buy into a cooperative, you buy shares in a corporation owning the building. In most cases, the number of shares you buy is based upon the size and location of the apartment. You receive a proprietary lease entitling you to use the common areas controlled by the corporation and, most important, to occupy the apartment. You are a voting member of the cooperative association and do have a voice in establishing certain common policies. You also pay a proportionate share of the corporation's property taxes, the current operating expenses, and mortgage payments.

As a rule, condominiums are easier to finance, buy, and sell, and there are fewer restrictions on the tenants. There is a wide variety in the sizes, locations, and prices of both condominiums and cooperatives on the market. To assume all of them are high-priced is erroneous.

Well, I certainly have the impression that co-ops and condos are expensive as a rule. My income will be going down in retirement. Who needs high or fast-rising carrying costs!

Carrying costs of a co-op or condo can be high, sometimes considerably higher than rental fees, depending upon the size and location of the property. A New York newspaper recently published an interview with a realtor, a middle-aged divorcee, who was quoted as saying she is happy her building is still rental because she does not want to pay high carrying costs. Yet some people seek to purchase condominiums or cooperatives because they want to own property. They like the idea of building equity, as well as knowing that where they live belongs to them.

That's fine when you have a choice. I just learned my building is going co-op. I am completely uninformed about co-op conversions and my rights. I have occupied my premises for more than twenty years. Now I am widowed. What do I do about competent professional advice without incurring astronomical fees?

Along with the growth of co-op conversions has come the emergence of cooperative conversion attorneys. They specialize in assisting tenants who have received "Dear Tenant" conversion letters.

If you wish to engage the services of such an attorney, see if there is a lawyers' association that could recommend an attorney to you. Maybe a friend knows of a lawyer specializing in co-op conversions. Be alert to newspaper and magazine pieces quoting co-op conversion attorneys. It could prove worthwhile for you to make note of prominent names quoted in real estate articles or in articles about other professionals. For example, Sally wanted the best professional legal advice when her building went co-op. She knew she could not afford the services of the attorney quoted in a magazine article, but telephoned him anyway. Telling him her income was certainly too meager to obtain his services, she asked him if he would recommend someone whose service she could afford. He did.

That's one way to help yourself. There are other ways, too. For example, the tenants in my building banded together to hire an attorney.
Yes, that's a good approach, too, in this situation.

Pearl, a divorcee, came home one day to find an announcement from her landlord notifying that he intended to convert her rental building into a co-op. Shortly thereafter, a notice of a tenant's meeting to explore the ramifications of going co-op appeared in her elevator. Some of the tenants recognizing the complexity of the situation had united in calling the meeting. Their intention was for the tenants to examine the situation cooperatively in order to protect their best interests as tenants. They followed the philosophy that in numbers there is strength, also taking into account that costs could be kept manageable by collective representation. It also guarded against the confusion that could arise with thirty tenants acting individually. In the meeting, the tenants agreed to engage the services of a reputable cooperative conversion attorney. He not only answered their questions and cleared away their confusion about what was happening and what to do, but also represented them subsequently in negotiations with their landlord.

That's encouraging. However, I'm divorced and without large money reserves. My building is going co-op. I can't

WHERE TO LIVE 43

even raise the down payment, let alone worry about maintenance costs.

Several alternatives present themselves in this difficult situation. You could borrow the down payment from friends or relatives, if you are lucky enough to know people who might lend you money and charge you no interest or only a minimal amount. Annabelle did this when she found herself in the predicament where she had no cash reserve, too little collateral for a loan, and no place to move to because in her price range apartments were scarce. A relative advanced the down payment at a low interest rate. Then she found a roommate to share the apartment and help pay the monthly maintenance charge.

Of course, you can apply for a bank loan, but if you are without suitable collateral, your chances of receiving such a loan are slim. You can contact a consumer finance agency for professional advice. Bear in mind that a tenants' committee is an excellent avenue of information and assistance. If one exists in your building, add your participation. If not, start one. It can be an excellent network for support and caring involvement. You might just learn how to finance your apartment through a committee.

I've been single all my life. My income is at a high point right now. I have money put aside, and I can afford both down payment and maintenance costs. I still want the best financing possible. After all, who wants to give away hard-earned money?

If you are in the enviable position of not having to worry about money, you can easily investigate a diversity of financing opportunities. You can use your time to shop for money, meeting several potential lenders to find out what financing is available before shopping for a place to buy.

It is important that you rate your ability to finance a mortgage realistically. Under most of the new mortgage plans, monthly costs are subject to change. Take a hard look at your personal financial picture, and honestly evaluate your probable earnings over the length of the mortgage. Your income, present as well as projected, should be enough to cover gradually rising monthly payments. Some people also consider a savings cushion vital to help meet the possible shock of a sudden large increase. What is interesting, too, is that many middle-aged singles in upper income brackets find that a mortgage serves as something of a tax shelter. The interest is deductible from taxable income. That is why many condominium buyers borrow money to finance the purchase, even when they can afford to pay cash.

I moved from a spacious apartment to a one-bedroom co-op after my husband died. He wasn't around to protect me anymore, and my former neighborhood seemed to be getting less and less safe. I also thought the investment in a co-op would carry me into retirement. I bought my apartment for cash.

Since you had enough money to buy your apartment for cash, you did not have to worry about mortgages and high interest rates. Besides, you are still entitled to certain tax deductions as you build equity in your apartment. So you have gained some of the financial advantages. If in addition you have provided yourself greater security, maintenance ease, social advantages, and an investment potential, you have treated yourself kindly. You can decorate your apartment as you please, yet have no responsibility for exterior upkeep. For you there will be no lawns to reseed and mow, no gutters to clean, no trash barrels to set outside several times a week.

My problem is whether to sell or to stay. I could make a neat profit selling my desirable co-op. But I enjoy living near my grown children. I love my apartment, and there has been so much stress in my life, what with my wife ill for so many years, that I want to be easy with myself now. As a man alone, I want both male friends and woman companions in my life. Where I live now, I not only have the closeness of my children, but the opportunity to make the friends I want.

The housing market may fluctuate, but an apartment in a well-managed building in a prime location will always have value. Then, too, the most essential thing is the satisfaction of living where you are happiest. Can you place a dollar value on that?

But suppose I am forced to buy my apartment because my building goes co-op and I cannot afford to rent elsewhere. Rental apartments are scarce in my city.

Then do the next best thing: Look into growing communities outside the center city area that are still close enough for commuting. Maureen, a mature divorcee, did this and was happy with her decision. She worked in the city, but often stayed late for dinner or a night out.

Perhaps renting part of your apartment is a means of producing extra income to pay your rent.

If you are "forced" to purchase—because there is no other place to live, because the neighborhood is so familiar, or because where you live is so close to work that transportation expenses do not exist—then you might have to take a risk in today's high interest market. Some people, rather than assume a mortgage at a fixed high interest rate, opt for the sponsor's financing. For several years they pay the interest rate charged by the sponsor's plan. After that they shop for a new mortgage, hoping by then to find a lower rate. It is risky, but you could come out ahead if interest rates descend in those intervening years.

My friend purchased his co-op for less than some of the later buyers, because he lived in the building when it was converted to co-op status.

A tenant living in the building is entitled to first crack at buying the apartment if the building is converted to co-op status. The insider's price can be much, much lower than that paid by people who reside outside the building. People have been known to sell their insider's purchase rights and make a profit doing so. They sell these rights to an outside buyer for more than the inside conversion price. Buying at the insider's price could also mean a larger profit if you decide to sell later on in life. You will have paid much less for your apartment than you will probably be able to sell it for. Consider the possibility. You might be lucky enough to have the co-op market work for you!

I have heard that in some places people sixty-two years of age and up have senior privileges wherein they don't have to buy into their building if it goes co-op.
This is so in New York State, and it would be wise to check the law where you live. In 1979, New York State legislated that people aged sixty-two or over, having an annual income of less than $50,000 from all sources and having resided in the building as primary residents for two years prior to the distribution of the offering plan, may elect to remain in the building as rent-paying tenants if the building is converted to a co-op or condominium. The widow of a deceased occupant, if she is at least fifty-five years of age, has the same rights. Contact the appropriate state housing agency for information about your state.

I would like to play more. That's why I bought a share condo vacation site with a friend.
This was Herman's thinking, too. He purchased a vacation condominium with a former partner. It worked out well. First of all, it reduced the amount Herman contributed to the down payment and monthly maintenance. Secondly, it provided him with one-half of a two-bedroom condominium overlooking the blue Pacific. Right now both partners use the apart-

ment for vacations, but in the back of their minds is the idea that they have a terrific place for eventual retirement.

Buying Property Abroad

I've long dreamed of owning a retirement condominium on the French Riviera. My late husband and I loved speaking French and meeting people from different countries. We planned on having our vacation home there while he was still working. Now that I'm alone, I'm having second thoughts.

And rightfully so! Purchasing property in a foreign country is something that deserves special consideration. It requires referring to an international real estate attorney, the United States State Department, and the consulate or embassy of the foreign country under consideration, because special laws apply on both sides. Some foreign investments are stable, but sometimes one gets caught up in a political problem that cannot be foreseen.

Ham experienced this when he purchased a retirement condominium in Portugal in a development a reliable Swiss builder was promoting. Ham invested a sizeable down payment in a townhouse and was advised that he could take occupancy in a year. It took seven years instead—seven years of dollars spent and anxiety until he could have his dream. When the Portuguese government went socialist, squatters occupied Ham's partially completed condo. The Swiss contractor was denied permission to oust them and complete the work. Both the contractor and Ham petitioned the new government, but no amount of petitioning or negotiating could succeed until the Portuguese government finally stabilized and decided to honor contracts with foreign builders. Ham eventually got his condominium, but without seven years' interest on his down payment. So if you are thinking of purchasing in a foreign country, be cautious, well informed, and ready to take risks.

It's too late for me to be cautious. My husband and I bought a retirement condominium in Israel because we both speak Hebrew and love the culture there. I received the condo as my part of the divorce settlement. I intend to live in Israel one day.

In addition to the fact that a pleasant climate lures the retiree to foreign places, the fact that one can identify with the culture is another drawing card. Sometimes people who have visited a country often or lived there before decide to retire there. Some teachers, writers, artists, or other people residing in foreign lands prefer to retire there rather than in the United States. Americans have retired to Canada, Ireland, Mexico, Central America, Britain, France, Spain, Portugal, and Israel. However, you should not move without a couple of extensive visits to your chosen land first. Before deciding, also write or visit consulates or tourist offices here to gather information on taxes, economic conditions, immigration status, working papers, medical care, and other important matters. Consider the problem of inflation. Many countries have very high inflation rates.

My friend speaks French fluently and thought she might like to retire in Geneva. However, she decided to test the waters by subletting a condominium there for a year.

This reminds me of Janet. She, too, retired to Geneva. Even though she was welcomed in the tennis club by friends, she was soon very lonely. While she spoke some French, Janet was not fluent in the language and found it difficult to develop meaningful friendships. After a while, she reached the point where she rarely left her apartment. She became very depressed.

Communication can be a real problem in a foreign country. That's why testing by subletting is a good idea.

Another problem to bear in mind is that Medicare benefits cease once you're abroad. Your own insurance could be costly, unless the country you move to has a public medical system for which you are eligible. While some folks say getting older means getting better, it should also mean staying healthy.

How About a House?

I've had my fill of home ownership. I raised three children in a sprawling ten-room house. Now my children are grown, living away, and I am alone. It's time for something smaller and centrally located. I want a place that means less responsibility, lighter housekeeping, minimal maintenance, and an easier life in the years to come. But the

Where to Live

thought of putting my house on the market and having to deal with realtors and attorneys worries me. They are so sharp, and I'm a novice. I've never sold a house before.

Suzanne, a woman alone, worked through a similar problem. She enlisted the aid of home-owning business friends and neighbors and received sound advice from them on how to deal with realtors and attorneys. Then she listed her house with reliable brokers, large and small realtors who had been recommended to her. When she needed the services of an attorney to prepare the contract for the sale, friends who had sold their homes referred her to someone reliable. She spoke openly with the attorney, stressing that, as a woman alone, she was counting on him to protect her interests. The attorney came through like a best friend and pro. He was both efficient and caring.

Through another neighbor, Suzanne learned about a couple who conducted tag sales. Here lay the answer to the disposition of ten rooms full of furniture as profitably as possible. She contacted this couple, a teacher and a court secretary who, interestingly enough, were developing a new career for their retirement. They were using their middle years to test their success with tag sales. They had already successfully completed two other home tag sales before Suzanne contracted with them to dispose of the contents of her home on a percentage basis. Promising to advertise in appropriate newspapers and journals and to take full responsibility for the sale—with the exception of pricing some furniture, for which they needed Suzanne's input—they came through with flying colors.

Taking this approach made it possible for Suzanne to deal with the emotions of the sale as well as with the financial considerations. The contents of her home represented years of living, and she did not want an indifferent auctioneer to enter her home and dispose of its contents solely as money-earning objects.

Learn to be your own best resource. Ask friends and acquaintances for aid when you need it. If you want to dispose of the contents of your home yourself, read the advertisements in your local newspaper. See if others are conducting such sales. Read the signs posted in the supermarket and elsewhere around the neighborhood. Attend a few sales. Speak to the sellers. By seeing how others do it, you can learn not to be afraid to handle a sale alone, if that is what you wish to do.

That's what I intend to do. Money is precious to me—I work hard for it. I'm not about to pay a brokerage fee to a realtor. There are books in the library about selling your own home. I'll place ads in the right newspapers and save myself thousands of dollars in commissions. I have lots of business experience. I've been taking care of myself since my wife and I separated and I feel certain I can handle everything.

Pay special attention to screening potential buyers by telephone before showing your house. Ascertain if they are in a financial position to meet your price and if it is safe to admit them as strangers to your home.

As a woman alone, safety is essential to me. That's why I am planning to keep my house. When I come home late, I pull up in my driveway and go right in the door.

One important reason people choose to remain or move from where they live is the safety factor. For women alone in particular, convenient garage facilities are vital. Others who choose to own their own homes do so because they cherish the privacy a home affords. Still others speak of space and the lack of noise restrictions, or of the chance to have a garden. Others cite financial considerations in their decision to own. The practicalities of tax breaks, building up equity, appreciation in value, and a hedge against inflation are important to them. Then, there are homeowners who cite the appeal of belonging in the neighborhood, as well as having the right to tailor physical space to their taste and needs. Whatever the reasons you have, if they suit you, they are right.

The space I have is what's right for me. Where will I find enough space for my children to visit if I sell my house? My children bring me pleasure in my present lonely life. And when I have grandchildren, my house is spacious enough for them to stay over, too. Those are my priorities.

Priorities are personal, and so are needs. Modern-day living has created both problems and solutions for many middle-aged homeowners. People are choosing to live where and how they are for reasons already mentioned. Others are exchanging one type of home for another as their needs change.

A new type of house on the market features two master bedrooms. This was designed to meet different needs, taking into account the economic squeeze, the expanding singles' market, and the extended lifespan of older adults and retired people. The two-master-bedroom house makes it possible for relatives and friends to live together, share household expenses, and have adequate space for comfortable living. The typical floor plan of this house includes two large bedrooms of equal or near equal size, each with its own bathroom. In some homes, upon instruction from the buyers, the builder will add a third bedroom and a small den or sitting area to one or both of the bedrooms. This flexibility is possible when more than one person covers the cost of homeowning.

Ida and Esther, two widowed sisters, decided to live together under such an arrangement. They pooled their money and invested in a house with two master bedrooms because they preferred to live comfortably together rather than each taking on the financial burden of living alone.

Keep alert to innovations in housing. Be open to all possibilities. That way you stand the best chance of finding a house that fits just right.

As I did. I've always wanted to own a home. I am planning to retire in a few years, and I found what pleased me in the small-home market. I have always been single, and owning my own home will give me roots. That's becoming increasingly important to me.

The studio home, another concept in singles housing, has answered many single people's needs. The studio home is essentially the same as a one-room apartment with a bathroom, kitchen, and patio area. Many older people find it appealing. For one thing, it costs less, depending on location. In addition, the one-time exemption from capital gains taxes of home sales up to $125,000 has fed the market for smaller homes. Older people can now trade down to a smaller house without a heavy tax burden. It makes good sense. After years and years of work, people want things easier. They want to keep the money they have earned, rather than pay heavy taxes, and they want a place to put down roots as well.

I want things easier. As a widower, I can't wait to get done with homeowning. The increased costs of home ownership and the potential reduction in income when I retire are two reasons. I feel isolated living in a neighborhood of homeowner families. I want to live near other singles. I want convenient social opportunities in my life now.

Situations change. So do needs. Many people sell their homes for the reasons you mentioned. Besides those, a house requires constant upkeep, and most people want their retirement years to be easy ones. Moving to where one has greater social opportunities is common. Become a persistent reader of the housing section of your newspaper. Pay attention to advertisements in magazines directed to mature people. Tune into the recommendations of others who have made a change. That's how to learn about availabilities and possibilities. Then decide what suits you.

Retirement Communities

I know many single people who are buying into adult communities, often developments with both retired and nonretired folks, before *they retire. What makes these communities attractive?*

If you were to take a sampling of people who live in adult communities, both working and retired people, you would find consistent themes running through their answers. They speak of neighborhoods changing, of their friends and neighbors moving away, and of finding themselves isolated. They want to live with people of their own age. This happened to Doris, a divorcee, who found herself alone because her friends relocated. She worried about what would happen to her as the years went on. After much investigation, she decided to buy into an adult community where she would be near people of similar age and have the chance to make new friends.

Social and recreational opportunities are built into adult communities. Community centers and colleges in the vicinity commonly offer programs for people desiring more extended opportunities.

Some singles buy a house in an adult community. Others select apartments in multi-unit dwellings because there is even more opportunity for meaningful social contacts there.

Not only are most adult developments built for maximum ease and convenience in housekeeping and maintenance, but many states offer tax and financial advantages to mature people and retirees. Many adult communities are located in the Sunbelt states of Florida, Arizona, and California. The warm climate means less wear and tear on the body. Adults appreciate that, particularly as they enter the later middle and senior years.

I notice you distinguish between adult and retirement communities. What is the difference?

Many adult communities have regulations prohibiting anyone except adults to reside there. Sometimes the cut-off age is sixteen. Anyone under the minimum age is permitted to visit, but not to take up permanent residency. Both working people and retirees compose the tenant body of adult communities. Usually only retired people reside in a retirement community. Some retirement developments call themselves leisure villages, thus signifying a life of leisure and the work years at an end. Children and grandchildren are welcome as visitors but not permitted as residents. It is advisable to investigate the rules and regulations of any adult, retirement, or leisure community you are considering.

I'm all for leisure. As a matter of fact, I'm planning to retire in a few years and I'm looking into retirement communities. There's only me to think of now, and I'll be making a decision alone. What should I look for?

You should be able to afford to live in the areas you choose. The price of the unit or the rental is most important, as is the cost of food, clothing, entertainment, and transportation. The climate should be suitable and the environment pleasing. Opportunities for employment should be present in the event you choose to work.

Explain this a little more fully.

Investigate housing prices, rents, and the desirability of the locations when you look into adult housing. "The National Directory on Housing for Older People" is available from the National Council on the Aging, 600 Maryland Avenue, S.W., Washington, D.C. 20024. Send for a copy of the pamphlet "Tax Facts," published by the American Association of Retired Persons, P.O. Box 2240, Long Beach, California 90801. In this free booklet, the pertinent tax provisions of every state, especially tax concessions to senior citizens, are described. If you want information about local property taxes, write to the county tax assessor. If there is a local taxpayers' association, you might be able to get a candid evaluation of future tax trends.

Examine the health facilities and quality of medical facilities through the local county medical association. What is the standing of the community, compared to national standards, in terms of the number of doctors and hospital beds? If you need special medical treatment, is it available? If you have a health problem, write to the Office of Public Affairs, United States Public Health Service, 200 Independence Avenue, S.W., Washington, D.C. 20201, and inquire if the area you are considering has facilities for taking care of your medical problem. Order material about climate from the National Climatic Center, Federal Building, Asheville, North Carolina 28801. Finally, explore the recreational and cultural facilities available, what special rates and discounts for older citizens are in effect and where, and the costs of property and automobile insurance. Thoroughness will pay off!

You say nothing about the cost of gasoline and transportation. Many retirement communities require automobiles and, as a solo driver, I think housing costs are high enough, without the expense of a car eroding my budget.

Where cars are necessary, car pools are answers to the high cost of gasoline and the absence of convenient transportation. Some retirement communities offer courtesy car services to assist residents with shopping. They might schedule a trip to the supermarket on Wednesday, a trip to another shopping center on Friday, and transportation to still another location on a different day. Often, the community courtesy car will arrange special transportation for small groups in the development. Sometimes there is a town car service, much like a taxi service, if you must hire transportation. Be certain to ask what the rates are for such a service. If bus facilities are limited, get to know people in your community and arrange to share rides for shopping or recreation. That will reduce the cost of gasoline for the driver, always a welcome trade-off. Use your ingenuity to establish supportive assistance for your transportation needs. You will be surprised at your own effectiveness.

My problem is how to deal effectively with the high cost of alimony. I would need to work, if I retire, and I wonder if this is alien to the concept of retirement communities.

Many people seek part-time employment when they retire from their full-time job. (See chapter 5 on work opportunities in retirement.) Retirement communities neither encourage nor frown upon residents working. This is a personal decision. For example, Harry, an expert bridge player, gave bridge instruction in his development. He was hired by the social committee. Later he explored opportunities to teach bridge aboard cruise ships that sailed out of a nearby port. Sometimes he is away for weeks teaching bridge. What it boils down to is developing your resources, determining what services you could offer the immediate and outside communities, and making this known. It is something that many retirees are doing.

Another thing retirees are doing, if planning to move to adult communities, is exploring the population living there. The idea of a homogeneous age group with only older faces is unappealing to me. I enjoy the exchange of ideas that different ages afford. That way I stay young in mind.

Some adult and retirement communities are deliberately building for and marketing to a variety of ages in order to develop a mixed population. Both young families and older adults are welcome in town houses. Private patio houses are sold only to mature people without families, and club facilities in the patio section are open only to residents of that section. Multiple units within the development are for adults only. People from all age groups mix together in the township stores and at the major community center on the premises.

If it is the stimulation of ideas you want, be certain the community you are considering is convenient to adult schools, colleges, libraries, and entertainment facilities. Again, you can always help develop resources along these lines if you are moving to a new community. Form a committee. Set up a stimulating cultural, recreational, and learning program on and off the premises. Use the tremendous resources of all residents to start your program off.

Are the popular Sunbelt states—Florida, California, and Arizona—the only locations where I will find such developments? I am widowed and my children are scattered east, west, north, and south. What's there to choose from?

As a matter of fact, retirement communities are being developed all over, not just in the Sunbelt. Some of the best values can be found in Utah, Louisiana, South Carolina, Nevada, Texas, New Mexico, Alabama, and Georgia. Prices are low. Tax incentives abound. And the "pioneering" spirit is contagious.

Visit your library and bookstore to find out about retirement communities. Locate retirement books for ideas and locations that interest you. The travel bookshelves are good for facts and figures, too. You can also write to the Department, Bureau, Council, or Division of Aging, usually located in the capital city of the state you are interested in, for information and referral to other places and people. (You can locate the name and address for the states that interest you from the same agency in your home state.)

I'd like less agency-oriented information sources. I have been caring for myself all of my adult life. I know agencies just give clinical, impersonal information. What good is that?

Write to the chamber of commerce in the town you are considering for information about organizations you belong to, such as Kiwanis, Lions, Rotary, Masons, or trade unions. Start corresponding with members there. Ask your local church or synagogue for the name and address of the pastor, priest, or rabbi in the towns you are considering. From those sources you can get a personal evaluation of local facilities, living conditions, treatment of older citizens, and anything else pertinent to retirees. Work through friends and associates to track down names of people in locales that interest you. Inquire of them about health facilities.

I am interested in retirement communities that offer superior health care and skilled nursing. I have been single all of my life and have no children to assist me if I am ill.

Facilities are being constructed that offer the independence of a place of your own together with freedom from household chores. The responsibility of cooking, cleaning, and housekeeping belongs to a staff. Cultural and recreational opportunities are present and the adequate health care and skilled nursing you are interested in is available as well. Sources of information about such retirement facilities are magazines and periodicals addressed to mature people. The real estate section of your newspaper may also contain advertisements from such facilities. Write for literature. Pay a visit, too.

Rescue me from the rescue squad! There's enough for the future retiree to cope with without being depressed by the appearance of the rescue squad, which is so common in retirement communities. I nursed my late wife long

Where to Live

enough, and I don't want to be reminded of this by the frequent presence of ambulances.

Retirement communities are not for everyone. If you would not be happy in one, there are the other housing alternatives discussed earlier. Then too, you can choose a mixed-age community where the rescue squad will probably appear less frequently. What you state is a common complaint of retirement and leisure village residents. You can see how important it is to use your middle years, your work years, to explore options in housing as thoroughly as possible.

Sounds like a lot of work ahead for me.

The more you do now, the happier you will be later on.

Determining Where You Would Like to Live in the Years Ahead

Jot down your thoughts about where, how, and in what you would like to live after retirement from your present position. As a single, consider options that might provide shared housing, living alone, relocation, staying put in present quarters, community living, and other housing alternatives.

1.

2.

3.

4.

5.

6.

7.

8.

9.

10.

A HOUSING HIGHLIGHT:
You are a King by your own Fireside, as much as any Monarch in his Throne.
—MIGUEL DE CERVANTES

Housing Self-Inventory

Determining retirement housing is a series of decision-making processes for you, the single, in midlife. Choices become clearer as basic answers are established—answers based upon insight and self-understanding, housing facts, and potentially viable conclusions.

1. Do you prefer to live alone or to share housing? _____
2. The advantages of living alone are: _____
3. The advantages of sharing living quarters are: _____
4. The disadvantages of sharing living quarters are: _____
5. What is most important to you in terms of location? _____
6. What would you need in parking facilities? _____
7. What is important in terms of transportation? _____
8. What safety features do you consider vital? _____
9. How close would you like shopping facilities? _____
10. Do you prefer living primarily with people of your own age, or do you prefer mixed ages? _____
11. What availability of employment would be important to you? _____
12. What is the maximum you wish to spend on housing? _____
13. What other particulars will help you determine future housing? _____

A HOUSING HIGHLIGHT:
The snail, which everywhere doth roam
Carrying his own house still, still is at home,
Follow (for he is easy paced) this snail,
Be thine own palace, or the world's thy jail.
—JOHN DONNE

Help, Help—It's Everywhere!

We have discussed people-aid available in making knowledgeable housing choices. In addition, there are resources galore to help the single person make an informed decision. Charting or listmaking often provides clarity, and removes confusion. Continue the list started below for gathering pertinent information about the geographical area you might decide to call home.

Information Sources	To Be Learned From These Sources
1. Local chamber of commerce	1. Employment; cultural activities
2. Subscription for six months to the region's local newspaper	2. Weather; problems of the area; taxes; activities of interest
3. Visit the area two or three times before moving there—and stay over	3. Real, visible contact; a feeling for the area beyond that which the media can give you
4. Builders' advertisements in real estate sections of newspapers	4. Written information about housing
5. Magazines catering to mature adults	5. Advertisements by builders; articles about different areas
6.	6.

A HOUSING HIGHLIGHT:
There is no place more delightful than home.
—MARCUS TULLIUS CICERO

WHERE TO LIVE 67

Even Exchanges

As new communities develop, employment opportunities increase, since services to residents and products fundamental to living must be made available. Therefore, if you choose to move to a new community, employment possibilities and social opportunities could certainly materialize, depending on your initiative, insight, and needs.

Products and Services a New Community Must Provide	*This Is How I See Myself Fitting In*
1. _____	1. _____
2. _____	2. _____
3. _____	3. _____
4. _____	4. _____
5. _____	5. _____
6. _____	6. _____
7. _____	7. _____

A HOUSING HIGHLIGHT:
Home's not merely four square walls,
Though with pictures hung and gilded;
Home is where Affection calls—
Filled with shrines the Heart hath builded.
—CHARLES SWAIN

Prepurchase Tips for Home Buyers

The Federal Trade Commission offers these tips to home buyers to prepare them for the biggest purchase of their lives —a new home:

1. Ask at least three people who have bought from your builder what they thought of the service after closing.
2. Find out whether the home has a warranty, and check with covered home owners about their experience with warranted items.
3. Check with your local Better Business Bureau and with local building and licensing authorities for reports on your builder's reputation.
4. Check your builder's financial status by requesting a Dun & Bradstreet credit report through your bank or other subscriber.
5. Get all verbal promises in writing.
6. Attempt to have all repairs completed before closing.
7. If the builder does not offer a warranty, find out what warranty plans are available. How much do they cost, and what do they cover?
8. Before closing, request a thorough walk-through inspection, and make note of any repairs needed at that time.
9. Make sure all extras are written into your contract. What you see in a model home is not always what you get in your finished house.
10. Find out if you will be responsible for paying for new streets, sidewalks, sewers, and waterlines. What will you have to pay for trash pickup and water?

For more information on the Federal Trade Commission's tips for home buyers, write to the FTC, Room 272, Sixth and Pennsylvania avenues, NW, Washington, D.C., 20580, and request the pamphlet House Hunters' Inspection Checklist.

A HOUSING HIGHLIGHT:
Tis at sixty man learns how to value home.
—EDWARD BULWER LYTTON

3
Your Health

Where Do You Stand?

I've reached a point in life when I realize more than ever how important good health is. Years ago, I would hear of my mother's friends dying or having a stroke, but I couldn't identify with those eventualities. Now that I'm middle-aged, I can.

The meaning of mortality takes on a new perspective at different stages of life. When singles reach middle age, intimations of mortality are present more than years before. Good health should become more of a concern not only to preserve life, but to enable you to live as fully, actively, and comfortably as possible.

It is important to understand that aging and sickness do not necessarily go together. Consider that arthritis often hits at ages twenty-five to forty. Heart attacks are 50 percent higher in men thirty-four to sixty-five than among men over sixty-five. Diabetes is not uncommon in children. Cancer claims 44 percent of those who die before age sixty-five. Of the population sixty-five or older, ninety-six out of every hundred Americans enjoy good health. And one of the rewards people over seventy-five enjoy is the ability to resist bacteria and viruses.

Then why do some people fear getting older? My widowed sister is sixty-two and insists she has only ten good years left.

Sometimes singles concentrate on numbers rather than facts, and what they express is an attitude rather than information. A federal agency, the National Center for Health Statistics, reported that the average lifespan of midlife Americans now fifty years old has expanded to 78.1 years. Among older Americans, those now sixty-five can, on the average, expect to live to 81.7 years of age. White women, now fifty years old, can expect to live another 31.2 years, approximately six years more than white men now fifty. Nonwhite women now fifty years of age can expect to live to the age of 78.9, while nonwhite men can expect to reach age 73.0. In terms of physical aging, science has shown that people begin to need glasses in their forties; that taste buds start to lose their sensitivity after sixty; that hearing is most acute at age ten and may gradually dull after that; that after sixty, the sense of smell begins to decline; and that muscular strength diminishes by one percent a year after the age of thirty.

Physical changes are taking place, but the mind can be strengthened at any age. Senility, the loss of memory and mental ability, is not necessarily synonymous with old age. It can strike at age thirty-five as well as at seventy-two. Approximately one out of every one hundred Americans past the age of sixty-five is senile.

Certainly no one can predict the number of healthy years left, but instead of trapping yourself with chronology, free yourself to make the most of your life. Be like

Your Health

Joseph, a middle-aged divorced man, who feels his life is enriched by all the experience he has had and who insists he would not want to be twenty-five again. Or ponder the slogan "Getting older is getting better" heard so often today.

I agree. It is important to know the facts. For example, as a woman alone, I am disturbed by recent television commercials. One pushes the removal of age spots by a cream. Another urges you to hide wrinkles with medication.

People in midlife have become a popular market for advertising agencies seeking to sell clients' products. Unfortunately, some advertisers do much to negate the pleasures of getting older and capitalize instead on the insecurities of the middle years. Sometimes reference is made to the midlife crisis when people realize that there are more years behind than ahead. But realistically, if you ask yourself where your life is heading, it makes little difference to your sense of direction that you have age spots, wrinkles, or gray hair. Learn to ignore media pressures. This is especially important for middle-aged singles since a sense of aloneness can aggravate negative feelings about aging. One reason for this is that often there is no one close to share feelings about aging.

Sometimes awareness that older women outnumber older men spurs some competitive women to spend large sums on cosmetics and medications. Other people understand that beauty is ageless, that the real beauty is that which you feel inside. A New York newspaper interviewed several women whose hair turned gray in their late forties or early fifties. These women refused to dye their hair blond, brunette, or red. One remarked that her gray hair helped her feel real. Another commented that gray hair says a woman feels good about herself, that she is satisfied with where she is in life. Join those satisfied people. Learn to use your energy to focus on vital things such as establishing a health plan to keep yourself healthy, both physically and psychologically.

Take a look at the drugstore shelves. There are multiple constipation preparations as well as products to negate aging discomforts. If aging doesn't worry you, visiting your drugstore will move you rapidly in that direction.

Only if you let it. This is where knowledge pays off. Some of the drugs are useful. But what is more valuable is a personal health plan. A program of regular exercise, weight control, moderate drinking (if you drink), cutting down on smoking (if you smoke), and keeping in a positive frame of mind can do more than all the items on the drugstore shelves. Visit your doctor and dentist for regular checkups to detect any illness at early stages. That will help prevent problems from snowballing.

Speaking of problems, I saw an article in a New York newspaper, stating that widows outlive widowers.

You are probably referring to the article in the *New York Times* of July 31, 1981, reporting that men whose wives have died are much more likely to die within the next several years if certain conditions exist. In this study, conducted by Johns Hopkins University researchers, still married men in the same age group and women who had lost their husbands were reported to live longer than widowers who do not remarry. Remarriage appears to increase an unwed man's prospects for living longer. This study took twelve years to complete, and more than four thousand widowed persons were interviewed. While social scientists are not ready to draw specific conclusions from the study, one scientist observed that remarriage could lessen stress and increase longevity by removing the chronic, long-term problem of being alone.

No Extremes Wanted Here

I know people living alone who drink alone when problems are heavy. If they are drinkers in the middle years, they continue drinking when retired, especially if time hangs heavy.

Any excess is self-defeating. Extremes often denote desperation, and that especially works against people who are alone.

Calm and peace are necessary for solving problems. To relax before dinner by having a drink can be delightful. Some people sleep better when they enjoy a glass of sherry or wine at bedtime.

Drinking in moderation is no problem. But, if like some singles, you find yourself drinking to excess, it is time to apply the brakes. One way to do this is to examine what you are doing to yourself. Alcohol is a deceptive depressant. You feel a rapid high, which sinks to a low later on. While heavy drinking helps you avoid facing what is troubling you, it never solves your problems. Instead, excessive drinking complicates life, because it may add physical problems to the emotional or social ones that exist—problems with the liver, blood pressure, and functioning of the heart muscle. And what about the excess weight excessive drinking adds? Each drink contains calories that in midlife and later life get harder and harder to shed.

If you really are your own best friend and alcohol has become a problem, take a look at your life. Is it that you are alone—friendless or without family? Planning for the future and not being afraid to look at life squarely could help you to work out today's problems. Another measure to prevent excessive drinking problems is to change your drinking behavior. Elicit the help of organizations competent in combatting alcohol excesses, Alcoholics Anonymous, for example. If you live on the East Coast, the National Council of Alcoholism, Inc. at 733 Third Avenue, New York City 10017, offers a list of organizations in more than one hundred cities that provide treatment for alcoholism. If you are a woman residing on the West Coast and have an alcohol problem, the Woman's Alcoholic Coalition, San Francisco Bureau of Alcoholism, San Francisco, California, offers women alcoholics individual and group counseling, vocational guidance, and an education in nutrition, physical fitness, and money management. People do care and, if you care about yourself, it is possible to work out any problem as a result of your having become a lone drinker or an excessive drinker—or both.

Your Health

Since my divorce, I don't bother cooking. It's amazing how the weight keeps creeping up, with my diet of fast-food meals, frozen dinners, ice cream, cakes, and other sweets. Snacking is fun except when I get on the scale. Snacking keeps me company.

Whatever happened to human company? Wouldn't you prefer to make friends and enjoy new companionship? Divorce means change, but there is no need to change to negative habits. According to the Center for the Study of Aging and Human Development at Duke University in North Carolina, obesity is one of the four major causes of aging prematurely. Obesity is also linked with hardening of the arteries, diabetes, gout, stroke, heart attack, high blood pressure, skin disorders, liver malfunctions, bladder disorders, fatigue, muscle pain, and irritability. If these medical problems do not convince you, take inventory of how you are feeling emotionally. If the highs outweigh the lows and are fairly consistent, good. Otherwise, it is time to change, just as Julie, a widow, did when she was displeased with eating alone. She waged a campaign to interest widows in dining together by arranging a meeting place and bringing her plan to the attention of almost anyone she met. Eventually people who had been eating alone joined together and dined enjoyably.

Old habits rarely change. They are just aggravated by divorce. How comforting that pint of ice cream is, and how soothing that half pie is when I'm distressed or lonely.

But how welcome is that excess weight when you cannot button your skirt or have to move over your belt buckle? Remember, too, that as you approach retirement age or as you grow older, there is more danger of excess weight because you tend to engage in less physical activity. Less food is burned up therefore, and excess food taken in turns to fat. At sixty-five, fewer calories (the difference is approximately six hundred per day for men and five hundred per day for women) are required to maintain good health than at fifty-five. One solution is to eat smaller portions of your regular food. If you take the time to notice how thin people eat, you will find they sample and taste rich foods and often have dessert, but they rarely eat excessively. Another effective step is to substitute lower calorie foods for higher ones. For example, when Charles, a divorced man, wanted to lose weight, he substituted canned pineapple in its own juice for pineapple bathed in heavy syrup. Some people join a weight reduction group. They find double value in this, experiencing the supportiveness of the organization and the opportunity to make new friends to soothe and comfort them in times of trial and tribulation. Then there are those happy, positive people who rid themselves of excess weight by dieting intelligently and rewarding their success with a new dress or shirt, a day at the theater or some other meaningful treat.

I reward myself after a heavy day's work by getting into bed and taking my supper on a tray there. Since my husband died, I cannot stand eating alone. If I have a dinner engagement with a male or female friend, I eat well. When there's only me, I keep mealtime very simple.

"Only you" deserves better treatment than that. "Only you" deserves the best treatment in the world! Who is more important than you, and who should treat you more regally than you? While many reports about eating problems in midlife and retirement focus on weight control, there ought to be more reporting about life control.

Burt, once widowed and once divorced, worked out his lonely eating problem by ordering dinner from a neighborhood gourmet shop. They delivered a delicious meal that he would eat at his dining table, which he set properly for himself. There was no need to cook or shop after a hard day's work. Others alone work out a shopping schedule so that they spend a few hours on the weekend buying the week's food. Sometimes they cook and freeze several days' meals. The number of cookbooks about cooking for one has grown. Visit your bookstore or library for suitable ones.

Some people who live alone make a point of having a dinner party once or twice a month, thereby providing themselves company to shop and cook for. This was Kate's decision after she was widowed. She decided to continue the delightful parties of her married life. She felt she had been punished enough by her husband's untimely death and had no desire to punish herself further by denying herself those things that pleased her. Leo, who was divorced, joined a men's club and enjoyed new friendships and companionship at mealtime that lessened his fatigue after a day's work.

Studies show that people who eat properly feel younger and actually look younger. People who eat enough proteins, minerals, and vitamins have more vitality than people who do not. Also, some insurance statisticians show that people over thirty who weigh fifteen or twenty pounds less than the average live longer. People who think they are important treat themselves importantly. They balance their lives, not only with well-planned menus, but with well-planned, balanced living. Pleasure and elegant self-treatment are high on their priority lists. The word *fun* is basic in their vocabulary. They derive pleasure from supportive involvement with others. Or maybe they are helping themselves to grow through self-established self-education programs. They rarely use food to compensate for loneliness.

Since I've been alone, smoking has become an increasingly important outlet for tensions. I now smoke more than ever before, and that worries me.

Everybody needs constructive outlets for tension and that is why creative and physical outlets are more popular today than ever before. As people understand more and more about human behavior, they realize how important it is to work out tension, anger, and frustration. Middle-agers alone and retirees alone, because they may not have someone close to talk to, or because they dislike participating in social events alone, have to work hard at establishing positive outlets.

Smoking is a negative outlet, harmful, addictive, and expensive. Serious illnesses attributed to smoking are lung cancer, heart disease, emphysema, circulatory disorders, and chronic bronchitis. Studies have shown that heavy smoking contributes to premature aging and early death. The risk of sudden death is five times as high for heavy smokers as for nonsmokers. So, if you cannot stop altogether, cut down. If you need help, call on one of the many profit and nonprofit agencies featuring programs to eliminate smoking. One of the major television networks in New York City ran a daily program for a period of two weeks to help people cut out smoking. The only price to the smoker was the cost of electricity for viewing the program.

Keep alert to any means of helping yourself, and remember to compliment yourself once you do resume control on a job well done. Extra strength is needed to eliminate excessive smoking, since smoking habits are usually well entrenched. If you succeed in kicking the habit, reward yourself by continuing to add new pleasures to your life, such as redirecting the cigarette money to travel, materials for your hobby, new clothing, a movie, or a concert. Also, learn to share your feelings with others instead of bottling them up. Once you ventilate a problem, you are halfway toward the solution. Talk to trusted friends and relatives. Give them a chance to help you. You will be helping them, too, that way.

All Through the Night

Now that I am single, I've become a middle-aged insomniac. While the city sleeps, I fume. What will happen to me when I retire?

Why project? Concentrate your energies on working out present problems. Try to determine how you can give yourself a well-deserved night's sleep. Begin now to change your behavior and start working on the relaxed mood necessary for sleep.

What keeps you from relaxing? If you can pinpoint this, you are at the starting post of working out your problem. Is it the aloneness that divorce brings? Are you hanging onto resentful, angry feelings about how you lived or about what has happened to your life? Hanging on to negative feelings makes people miserable. Often people who cannot sleep prevent themselves from relaxing by using that time to mull over angry feelings. If that is the case, teach yourself to accept situations you cannot change. Learn to forgive and understand. Try keeping a notebook to record your thoughts and feelings. Find new friends or one really close one to whom you can talk intimately. Read yourself to sleep with something that relaxes you. And ask yourself if you are giving yourself enough fun in your present life. Finally, a visit to your doctor, if you have not done so already, could shed more light on your problem.

I've become a night owl since my husband died. I'm embarrassed by this. Maybe I should retire to China, where my present hours would fit in fine.

Sometimes people need a reason for waking up early. Perhaps it was breakfasting with your mate that provided you the impetus to get out of bed. If that impetus no longer exists, you'll find you need to provide yourself with a new one. Otherwise there is little motivation to pursue a new pattern of behavior. Finding a job or making a commitment for volunteer work provides a schedule or structure that many people need. Practice patience as well as effectiveness so that you learn to take it easy with yourself as you change your behavior. Set your alarm and push yourself out of bed in the morning. Try complimenting yourself as you succeed in your new behavior. Do not take long naps during the day; catnap instead. This will refresh you without interfering with your night's sleep. Finally, keep your sense of humor. Sometimes it is hard to laugh or to laugh at yourself when you feel out of control, but in due time everything is possible.

Time! I'm in bed late and up late in the mornings. Am I a night owl, too? If so, I don't mind. I'm a single male and my own boss. I'm in real estate. I make my own hours and often I don't fall asleep until 3 A.M.

Habits and patterns that are pleasing and productive are just what the doctor ordered. If your life works for you, fine.

One problem with singles who have sleeping problems is that they are dissatisfied with their lives. Another problem is that they do not get enough exercise. Perhaps physical conditions such as noise or other irritations interfere with sleep.

Mature people who accept themselves, who are not fearful or defensive, and who choose to do their best and trust themselves to do just that rather than worry have an easier time relaxing and sleeping. It is a way of saying, "I am satisfied with myself?" This is not a smug or pompous feeling, but a sense of well-being that permeates people at peace with themselves. These are easy people to be with, people who are accepting of themselves and others. They are people who usually find humor in everyday things. That is different from forcing a cheerful frame of mind on yourself before falling asleep. For if the cheerfulness is discordant with usual feelings at bedtime, it may still keep you from falling asleep.

I don't know why I'm an insomniac. I've cut out caffeine, and still I don't sleep. This problem has grown worse since my wife died. What with the long hours I put in working, I would think I would be exhausted and fall asleep easily.

One theory about insomnia is that it is related to depression and anxiety. What is interesting is that sleeplessness can engender more sleeplessness, rather than provide rest for the weary.

Clint, a widower, developed an insomnia problem after his wife died. He worked an exhausting schedule, cut out caffeine, and tried falling asleep to the whisper of soft radio music, but nothing worked. One thing Clint missed was a close friend, which was what his wife had been. He sorely needed someone to confide in, to help him understand how he could put the pieces of his life together, but he was not ready for closeness with a member of the opposite sex. He had more mourning and healing left to do. So he found a supportive friend, Max, who helped by listening to his problems. When he could share his anxieties, Clint's insomnia problem eased.

Perhaps others in midlife who are alone could similarly help themselves sleep better by finding a close friend, male or female. It could mean someone to care about you and someone for you to care about. It could show you that you are not alone. It could be self-renewing, because you would be teaching yourself to rebuild an important part of your life and learn to trust again. In addition, it could provide some happiness in your life while you are rebuilding.

Unfortunately, the reasons for insomnia are still poorly understood by medical science. But rest assured that medical and psychological research is concerned with sleeplessness, because it is common in adults and commonplace in the elderly. While the scientists are engaged in finding ways to help the poor sleeper, find ways to help yourself, too. Your close friend will not always be available, so try reading yourself to sleep. Enjoy a glass of sherry before bedtime to relax you. Lull yourself to sleep with soft music.

How Do You Spell Sex?

What chance does the single middle-aged woman have for sexual fulfillment, what with the ratio of older women to men so much greater?

It is a real problem and there is no easy solution to recommend. Sex is something very private and personal, so you will have to seek your own answer. If sexual fulfillment is not possible, whether due to numbers or religious beliefs, substitute outlets such as sports or creative activities. It certainly does not measure up to a pair of warm arms or the human touch, but it may ease some of the tension.

The tension I feel is not due to the lack of sex but to the pressure older women apply today. Maybe it's the sexual revolution. I don't know. As a recently widowed man, I would enjoy friendships with women, but most of them want a sex partner.

Middle-aged men function differently. Harry, a widower, considers himself a very sexual person. He is pleased that women find him attractive and happy that they make advances to him. Alf, retired and divorced, says that women should distinguish between the sexual experience and a deep relationship. He insists women often read into the sexual encounter what they would like in terms of a long-term relationship, rather than in terms of what is actually there. Salvatore, a widower, maintains that women look to snare him into bed primarily because they hope to keep him permanently attached. David, a widower, enjoys the sexual experience but encounters potency problems from time to time.

Potency seems to be a problem with more and more middle-aged and older men. They come on strong and then have problems with the sex act. As a single woman, I don't know what to make of it.

For both men and women, widowed, divorced, or separated, it is quite difficult to enter the dating world after a lifetime of marriage. The demands of the singles world can be overwhelming. Of course, establishing a working friendship is always a good foundation for any relationship. According to some singles, if the sexual attraction is there, that union will eventually take place later, unpressured and without tension or anxiety. Others say that waiting only increases the tension.

As for impotence, this is something for people in the medical and psychological field to address in depth. One barrier to overcoming or treating impotency is a man's reluctance to admit his problem, to speak about it to people close to him or to professionals. In the macho society our middle-aged and older men were raised in, one prime characteristic of masculinity was potency, and bragging about sexual successes to other men and women is common with some men. That does not always mean that words and actions coincide.

Since I've been a widower, I've had sexual problems. Naturally, if my wife were alive, we would try to work it out. But I'm certainly not going to talk to strangers as in sexual encounter groups and groups that endorse letting your feelings hang loose.

The first logical step in working out sexual problems is to talk to your physician. Most people in midlife or older have a doctor they feel comfortable with. If the problem is not physical, other remedies are available, such as counseling. Sexual drive and sexual activity can be a continued source of pleasure as one grows older, particularly since the pressures of work have been removed.

It is important to treat sexual problems early. This can work to your advantage, preventing additional physical stress and psychological anxiety by keeping matters uncomplicated. Hopefully, the treatment you decide upon will work. If it does not, find another way to work out your problem. What works with one man may not work with another. For example, one recent study found that an exercise program through which the overall level of conditioning improved, resulted in more sexual activity on the part of the men. If such an exercise program is risky for you because of a heart condition, participate in a limited program instead. And always remember that you are a worthwhile person. See yourself as a total man, to help yourself enjoy all the richness and fullness of life.

That's what I'm trying to do—enjoy myself. But as a widow, I am annoyed with the attitude of some older men. They've taken on the kids' role, and some of them have adopted the Kinsey Report as gospel. I'd like to be friends with single men, but most of them don't permit this.

Older women who have male friends say they have arrived at this point through communication. They talk about what they want—really talk. Then, if a common ground can be reached and both want the same type of relationship, fine. When goals differ, these women accept that and move on to explore relationships with other people. It boils down to live and let live, rather than manipulate.

Energy: Getting It, Using It

As a woman who's always been single, I put a great deal of energy into work. As a result, I have worked my way up the corporate ladder. The pressures are tremendous, but then again, so are the pleasures. I don't want to sound conceited, but I have become a champion ice skater. It's a wonderful way to let off steam and answer my physical needs.

Every single needs a positive outlet, and exercise is one way to let off steam and remove fatigue, too. Not only does exercise strengthen muscles, it has other valuable results, too. It improves posture, benefits circulation, and also encourages deeper breathing. Look at people who exercise! You will see a glow to their face and skin. They look as though life has touched them with a special radiance.

Life has touched me, but in a way I don't like. I was widowed recently. I find myself tired now, more than ever before in my life. I feel depressed. I don't have anyone around to tell me how wonderful I am, and the search for this kind of personal support is exhausting.

Fatigue and depression are interrelated. That is one reason mental health professionals advise people living alone to develop their inner resources and to live their lives as richly as possible. It helps recharge one's batteries. Developing a career, interests, and hobbies or volunteering to help others are ways of telling yourself how wonderful you are. That is what is meant by utilizing your own inner resources to create a productive life for yourself.

Get out and do something important. If finances are a problem but you can work, look for a job that can create opportunities to do something rewarding and to hear how well you are doing. If finances are not a problem, experience that inner glow from volunteer work. Help a child learn to read. Do publicity for a local theater company. You will be amazed at how much energy returns when you step away from your immediate problems. Yes, you will still feel the loss of your mate, but dwelling on what you do not have instead of on what is presently available keeps you a victim rather than someone who has control of his or her own life. Learn to let off steam. Reenergize.

My idea of letting off steam is playing tennis. When my husband was alive, we played tennis together. Now that I am alone, I find tennis a particularly marvelous outlet, and I've made friends at the tennis courts, too.

An important criterion in selecting exercise is to choose to do something you enjoy. Formal calisthenics are not the only type of exercise that will help you lose weight or perk you up. Any physical activity you enjoy, recreational or otherwise, will satisfy you. If it pleases you, you will go back to it. If not, like Dita, a widow who joined an exercise class and was soon bored with it, you will quit or participate less enthusiastically. Vera, a divorcee, loved to dance. She joined various dance groups at her local community center, including one for ballroom dancing in which the men circulated among different partners—the women were not pressured to bring along a male escort. Some people like to rediscover a previous favorite sport, such as swimming, playing golf, ice skating, riding, or bicycling. Others enjoy learning a new sport.

Whether you are a beginner or advanced, experiencing the joy of using your body is refreshing. Walking is wonderful exercise because it keeps your mind bright and alert as it tunes up your body. It is something you can do alone and inexpensively. Walking increases the flow of oxygen to the brain. Some physicians maintain you can lose ten pounds a year just by walking a mile a day. If you feel pleasure, exercise. If you feel angry, exercise. Work off steam. Walk. Run around the block. Join an exercise class at the Y. Many local centers are designing exercise programs for people who are single and fifty-plus. Go find yours!

One simple way I contend with harmful feelings is to hammer away at a sculpture I am working on. It is a hobby I enjoy, and anytime I feel tense and angry or annoyed at my separated wife's heavy alimony demands, I turn to my sculpting and feel better.

Coping is to your credit. If you feel mentally overloaded, take time out. Go for a fifteen minute walk. Read a book. Visit or phone a friend you have not spoken to in some time. Play your guitar. Do something you do not ordinarily do.

Some singles, when they feel frustrated or angry, burn the person they are angry at. No, they do not actually set fire to the individual. Rather they write that person's name on a slip of paper, then burn that paper in an empty coffee can. It is remarkable how much relief that simple process brings, especially if there is no one around to talk out your feelings to.

I find rap groups a wonderful way of renewing energy. I enjoy them as a way of sizing up situations about different people and expressing what's on my mind. Rap groups are marvelous tension relievers.

It's important that you find some way to relieve tension. Tension creates a stress reaction in the body. Stress can make body organs function less efficiently; it causes faster aging. Stress is believed to cause high blood pressure, heart attacks, cancer, arthritis, diabetes, ulcers, and kidney trouble. Since these effects accumulate over the years, stress can be particularly harmful in the middle years or during retirement. Harmful emotions—resentment, frustration, fear, anger, annoyance—result from stressful situations. A certain amount of stress is normal, but it needs to be relieved regularly. So if you feel resentment, or some other tension-inducing emotion, learn to talk it out. Rap groups are one way to do this. Join such a group or form one yourself. Let good feelings in. Send bad ones out.

The Doctor Connection

I'm constantly receiving mail about one health insurance policy or another. I need help deciphering most of the material. I wish all those people so anxious to help me protect my health would wait until I ask them. Sure, I know I should be certain to have enough health coverage now that I am single, but pressuring me is not going to result in my buying another policy.

Protecting yourself with medical and hospitalization coverage is extremely important for the midlife single. Because hospital costs have spiraled, many singles are seeking group coverage through business or professional and other associations. Group coverage usually means lower premiums. Sometimes it is possible to convert from an existing group policy to individual coverage when you retire. You are usually granted a limited amount of time to make this conversion and thereby assured uninterrupted coverage. The cost of the premiums is usually much higher, however.

Most important is to decide what kind of coverage suits you best. For example, are you satisfied with the limited choice of doctors some plans offer, or do you prefer to choose your own doctor from a wider circle? How much does the coverage cost? How does it compare with other similar plans? What specifically are you covered for?

If you are deluged with mail from companies offering coverage to people over fifty, ask yourself what they are offering that would help you. If the policy features extended hospital coverage above and beyond what your present policy covers, determine exactly what the extra benefits are. Then speak to your physician or knowledgeable friends about adding such coverage. While some people say most hospitals discharge patients as quickly as possible, others maintain that supplementary insurance is a must for any possible long confinement.

The decision is yours, of course. But try to make the decision with insight and information.

Other questions about health insurance policies are: On what day of hospitalization does the policy take effect? How much extra does it cover? Does the premium warrant investing in the policy? What precisely does the policy cover? Do not be taken in by an emotional pitch delivered by mail or television advertising urging you to act immediately. Even if the companies are applying pressure, you do not have to pressure yourself.

Illness is expensive both in terms of dollars and emotions. I know this from my late husband's bout with cancer, which lasted two years.

Cost of quality medical care is a major concern to everyone. There are ways of reducing costs without sacrificing proper care, such as preventive medicine. Some expensive health problems result from personal habits. Cardiovascular, lung, and liver diseases are often linked to chronic stress, excess weight, diet, heavy drinking, or smoking. Cancer can sometimes be detected and easily managed by early and regular checkups.

But if you are not so lucky and have to go to the hospital, is there a way to cut down costs?

Instead of visiting the hospital emergency room for routine health matters, see a doctor. The saving could be from one-third to one-fourth of what you would pay the hospital. For elective surgery, get a second opinion, and inquire about the fees, too. Do not leave questions here unspoken. Another surgeon's fees could be less for the same operation. Also, if it is the type of minor surgery that can be done on an outpatient basis, the costs could be $100 to $300 less, depending on the operation and the number of hospital days eliminated. Since hospital confinement can be very expensive, try to have tests done on an outpatient basis whenever possible. Most important, if you are single, to keep hospital expenses manageable be certain your coverage is in effect and adequate.

Doesn't Medicare help with health coverage?

Medicare helps pay health costs for those sixty-five or over or disabled. It includes hospital insurance for inpatient care and certain types of follow-up services, plus medical insurance to help pay doctors' bills, outpatient services, and other medical items. There is a monthly premium for the medical insurance. Hospital insurance coverage can begin at sixty-five, even for those who are not retired. Visit your Social Security office to file for Medicare at least three months before your sixty-fifth birthday, whether or not you will continue working. Your Medicare card will then be sent to you. If you cannot visit the office, write or telephone for instructions.

For your information and reference, the Social Security Administration has a booklet describing precisely what Medicare does and does not cover. The booklet is free. Send for a copy so you can know what your rights are. Remember, too, to keep alert to changes in Medicare coverage, since costs of premiums and deductibles you pay are subject to occasional change.

I am a widowed physician, and recently I underwent heart surgery. Knowing how expensive hospital internment is, I've made it a practice to carry extensive insurance. A history of repeated illnesses was another reason I covered myself extensively.

If only we could predict the unpredictable, how orderly this world would be. Yes, the unknown is something singles must contend with. Since it is impossible to predict if and how much medical care you will need, a guide for determining coverage could be previous medical history, family history, or simply what you can afford in medical premiums.

Some people say doctors who are members of medical plans are not as good as doctors in private practice. Supposedly, the reason these doctors associate with medical plans is because their practice doesn't earn enough for them.

Some medical plans permit patients to select their own physicians and thus use doctors in private practice. Other plans insist you use their group's doctors, so your choice is limited. Whether referring to a private physician or a group doctor, the patient should feel respect and have a rapport with his doctor. Ruth, a widow, went through two mastectomies in which her group doctor operated. She had sufficient income to engage a private physician and understands what qualifications to look for in physicians, as her sons are doctors. However, she maintains that since all doctors must pass medical boards, the group's physician is as qualified as any other physician.

Who can really tell the score? I was certain my wife would outlive me because I have a heart condition. She died five years ago of fast spreading cancer. Here I am today alone.
No psychic, no physician, no researcher can predict the future. Even the best medical advice is ineffective for forecasting the future. To do the best you can, live as much as possible while you are alive. To enjoy good health and its blessing as long as humanly possible is all you can expect of yourself.

Let's change the subject a little bit. Let's talk about good health rather than illness. Funny I should say that—I'm a single, middle-aged man, balding and distressed about losing my hair.
Maintaining the body in good health is so important. Proper diet can keep the skin fresh and glowing. Exercise helps, too. But there are cautions to observe. For example, overexposure to the sun may produce brown, scaly patches on your face, hands, and arms. It may also induce skin cancer. Be sure to check your eyes regularly and avoid eye strain. Care for your feet with daily bathing, massage, and the proper foot coverage—socks, properly fitting shoes, and rubbers when needed. Neglecting your feet can lead to other body disorders.

Practice good posture. This will counteract the natural weakening of the back muscles that many middle-agers experience as a result of inactivity, poor posture, and tension. Good posture will make you more attractive, too.

Keep your teeth in good condition. Eat sensibly, and visit your dentist on a regular basis. This is particularly important once you reach middle age, because your teeth can reflect a lifetime of problems.

Give your heart a break and the support it needs by keeping your weight down, cutting down or eliminating cigarettes, getting enough sleep or rest, exercising regularly, and minimizing tensions.

As far as your hair is concerned, there is no medical prescription or technique to prevent it from graying or falling out. Going bald is a matter of inherited characteristics.

Your Health

Building Health and Fitness in Midlife Through Retirement

Continue this list of positive steps for dynamic fitness now and in the years ahead. Life expectancy can be increased by an optimum physical and mental health program.

1. Moderate use of or abstain from alcohol.
2. Don't smoke.
3. Avoid heavy snacking between meals.
4. Stay within 10 percent of your proper weight.
5. Have a regular exercise program.

(Add your own.)

6.

7.

8.

9.

10.

11.

12.

13.

14.

HEALTH HELPER:
Most folks are as happy as they make up their minds to be.
—ABRAHAM LINCOLN

4

Leisure for a Lifetime

Looking Leisure in the Face

At work, I feel important. I have a place to go to everyday; I have friends and a salary that covers my expenses. It upsets me to think of losing all of this when I retire, and I wonder how good I'll feel about myself, especially since I'll have so much time alone.

Time is not the problem. Attitude is. Try focusing on retirement as a transfer—a transfer of hours from toil to hours of leisure—and redirect your energies from making a living to living well. In this transition, see yourself reallocating time. Explore how leisure can replace the gratification work supplies. At work you receive recognition. You have status and financial security. You have a place to go, day in and day out. In addition, you have made friends that you see workdays and weekends. You can enjoy similar gratifications in retirement. Retiring assures you the freedom of going where you want, traveling as you please, making new friends of your choice, and involving yourself in activities you select. You can fill leisure hours with challenges, excitement, growth, exploration, and fun.

It sounds as if leisure is a lot of work. Besides that, I'm more concerned with worthwhile activities than I am with just filling time. After all, how many times can I go to the theater?

As often or infrequently as you like or can afford. You see, the key word in leisure planning is *balance.* In your work years, you are balancing your life with work, recreation, family, and friends. If your life consisted only of work, you would soon be exhausted, mentally and physically. In retirement, balancing leisure can mean a combination of activities: simple fun, exposure to new ideas, making new friends, service to the community, exercise, and hobbies, which many people develop into careers. To do justice to a leisure program, particularly in retirement, when leisure hours are plentiful, you need to understand what leisure is all about, to learn to make choices that will make you feel good, through giving to yourself, to others, or both.

Picking and Choosing

I don't know where to start, except to continue what I've been doing with leisure hours all along. I've seen singles flit in and out of leisure activities, spending a lot of money and time. I know singles who do nothing but sit in front of the television for endless hours. It's difficult when you are alone and have no one to spur you on. I suppose it'll get even more difficult in retirement.

It may, but you can make it easier by taking inventory of what is available and what appeals to you. For example, if making new friends is what you wish, engage in volunteer work or group social activities. Consider working with organizations like the International Rescue Committee. Learn to play bridge or take up a sport, such as tennis or bowling. If you enjoy working with your hands, think about getting instruction in art or a handicraft that appeals to you. Tutoring children might be another way of providing yourself with a sense of self-gratification.

If recognition is what you like in retirement, try developing your latent acting skills in a little theater group. Investigate participation in a "swap-meet" situation—an informal teaching set-up in which you "trade" any special knowledge or ability you have with others who later share their special interests at other "swap-meet" times. Or if a commitment is what you want to help you feel secure and worthwhile, how about taking credit or noncredit courses with other adults sharing in similar interests? That can result in having a place of interest to go to week in and week out. If you have a passion for books, join or organize a book club, and make sure it meets regularly. Regularly scheduled activities can do much to provide that secure feeling going to work used to provide.

I never thought about my leisure time. I just did as I pleased, sometimes planning, sometimes not.

You get more mileage out of leisure when you develop a strategy for selection of leisure activities. You have a better chance of involvement in pursuits that appeal to and have meaning for you.

Some people use a kind of self-inventory to decide what they really want to do. They ask themselves questions like "Do I prefer working with others or working alone?" For example, if they prefer being with others and have an interest in painting, their choice might well be taking a class at the local community center. If, however, they prefer working alone, you might find them high on a windy hill, keeping company with only a canvas.

Another question people often ask themselves is "Do I have a special taste for pets?" Bob, a divorced middle-ager, took up raising dogs in retirement, something he had yearned to do most of his working life but could not pursue in the city. People who enjoy working with their hands have many choices available to them, such as gardening or growing indoor plants. People who enjoy collecting things might start with autographs of famous people, button collections, or coins.

Lovers of the outdoors have many options, including a lot that are quite inexpensive. Birdwatching, hiking with a sports club, and nature walks can provide hours of leisure fun.

People who enjoy being specialists might choose to study a language or join a wine tasting club. Eddie, a widower, was invited to join just such a club. At each monthly tasting, a different member took responsibility for selecting the wine and preparing a menu and program relating to the region where the wine was grown. For his turn, Eddie selected a Swiss wine, prepared a fondue menu, and presented a slide-illustrated talk about the region in Switzerland from which the wine was imported. If this appeals to you and there is no wine club where you live, start your own. Most wine shops will gladly assist in getting your group well started.

Is there anything in particular I should take into account now, in my work years, for when I retire alone?

Yes, consider your freedom to explore interests now an advantage to put to immediate use as fully and richly as possible. Perhaps right now you feel you lack the time to do the things you'd like. Start just with picking up information about possible interests. When you do retire, you will have much more time. You will already have a good sense of how you want to fill that time. Maybe you will be one who boasts, "There aren't enough hours in the day to do everything I want to do!" How much better that is than complaining of empty hours you don't know how to fill.

School Days

I would enjoy using some of my leisure in educating myself further. I'd like to enroll in college, but I would feel foolish among younger students. Then, too, I have doubts about my capacity for concentrating, after so many years away from school.

It is natural to have doubts, but focus on the positive rather than the negative. Concentrate on the fact that schooling is an excellent source of intellectual stimulation and growth, as well as a possible starting point for new careers. As a fringe benefit, school offers a potential source of new friendships to fill those hours alone.

College officials are generally aware of the unsureness of returning adults and commonly provide special programs to assist the mature student. For example, there are study groups organized by college counselors strictly for returning adults. Some colleges have "encore clubs" for students who started studying for a degree years ago but had to drop out before graduation. "Encore clubs" are support organizations designed to help returning adult students succeed in their studies. So welcome are mature adults on college campuses that many schools award them life experience credits. In general, mature students are welcomed by administration, faculty, and other students, because they are virtually always studious, cooperative, and self-motivated.

Could we get back to life experience credits for a moment? I'm not sure I know what that means.

Some colleges award academic credits for work and life experiences. It's a way of recognizing the education you've gained through career and personal endeavors over the course of the years. Being awarded these credits shortens the amount of time and money required to earn a degree. Usually the office of the dean of admissions at your school can inform you about life experience credits and how to apply for them.

I want an easier, more fun way of learning. After all, I will have spent enough demanding years at work.

There are many options for the mature single returning to school. You don't have to make it any more difficult for yourself than you want. You can enroll on a degree or nondegree basis, or even on an auditing basis. Again, the office of admissions of the college of your choice is the source to contact for information. Make an appointment; ask for the college bulletin listing courses offered. Many universities have special programs for adults who want to pursue educational opportunities without worrying about credits or grades. In some schools a division of life-long learning or continuing education has been established specifically as the information source for noncredit work. It is also often possible to audit or attend and observe courses without formally registering. The appropriate department chairman is usually the person to contact here. You are allowed to sit in on lectures without having to be concerned with examinations or credits.

It still sounds too demanding. I can apply myself to topics or subjects I am interested in, but I don't want to get involved with a lot of academics. Is there any other way?
There are several other ways, but however you do it, do it with commitment. Remember that taking courses is one of the best ways to replace the structure you found so valuable at work and to bring meaning to your extra leisure hours alone.

As for a less demanding way, see how some of these suit you: an adult education (or, as it is sometimes referred to, a "continuing education") course in French or finance. Or you can be with other adults as you learn to repair clocks, study Cantonese cooking, or exercise away excess pounds.

"Swap-meets" were mentioned earlier. At "swap-meets" adults exchange and share their own specialties, usually arranging to do so in a community center or on a college campus. For example, if, like Steve, you are a skilled photographer, you could instruct a small group in photography technique. Sally, whose specialty might be wood sculpting, would, at a later date, instruct a small group in that.

Still another approach to learning is through the Institute for Retired Professionals. Members are retirees interested in sharing their knowledge and in perpetuating their own intellectual and social growth by teaching courses and lecturing to other retirees. The contributions each makes depends on his or her areas of expertise. These institutes are housed on college campuses and sponsored by the college. Inquire of colleges in your area whether they sponsor an institute or otherwise know of a school that does. I have heard retirees praise the fine courses and lectures they have attended in subjects like architecture, psychology, and engineering. As a bonus, for a small membership fee, you can audit a number of credit courses at the college, too.

There's a lot to choose from. Where did I ever get the notion that spending my later years alone meant that I would have to be lonely?

Fortunately, now you know otherwise.

Here is another valuable possibility for you to investigate: Elderhostel, an innovative senior citizen educational program that in eight years has grown to include six hundred colleges and universities in fifty states. You can combine education and travel in an Elderhostel program that provides one-week sessions of education and recreation for retirees sixty-plus on campuses both in the United States and abroad. Write for information to Elderhostel, Suite 200, 100 Boylston Street, Boston, Massachusetts 02116. If you are younger than sixty, New York State's Senior Seminar Program is a similar group for young folks, fifty-plus. For information, write Senior Seminar Programs, Skidmore College, Saratoga Springs, New York 12866. Many other states have similar programs.

Rough Weekends Ahead?

Weekends are the loneliest for me. I'm certainly not going to be attending school Friday night, Saturday, or Sunday.

So use those weekend hours to exercise, socialize, and pursue your hobbies. Many singles in their middle years or older use leisure weekend hours to develop personal interests. Take a look at Gary, a certified public accountant who used his free time writing feature stories about finances and taxes for leading singles' magazines. It provided him a second career in free-lance writing. He expects to write even more after retirement from his full-time job.

Speaking of exercise, I think of future years alone with no one to confide in and that makes me feel tense. Would using leisure hours to exercise be one way of coping?

It certainly would be. Or a good session in woodworking or throwing paint on a canvas might be other solutions.

Studies have indicated that 60 percent of people over sixty can do pretty much anything they want, as far as exercise possibilities go. So why not actively employ those leisure hours for fun, tension relief, and good health? If you prefer organized exercise sessions, check out your local Y. Many Y's offer afternoon, evening, and noontime classes in exercise for people fifty-plus, as well as dance instruction in folk, social, flamenco, Scottish Highland, ballet, aerobic, and tap dancing. If you prefer sports, try letting off steam with swimming, golf, tennis, archery, walking, or the latest fad, jogging. Any kind of exercise will do the trick. The criterion many singles recommend for deciding which activity to take up is that the exercises express how you feel about your body and yourself. If you are motivated, nothing will stand in your way—just as nothing bars Dorothy from walking around the park while her friends jog. She enjoys walking and is respected by her jognik companions for her daily exercise commitment, weather permitting.

Freedom, F-R-E-E-D-O-M!

I feel better now and more together. I guess there is a real freedom in being single. Maybe retiring alone can provide pleasure for me if, as you suggest, I think positively and use my leisure time to my advantage.

That is precisely the philosophy of the mature singles' social networking group, Royal IMPS, or In-Mature People, located at 235 East 57th Street Suite 4B in New York City, 10022. Start simple—start *now* in your middle years, *before* you retire. Explore options. Ask yourself, "What would give me the most pleasure if I had extra time to spend?" Make your selection on the basis of interest, time, budget, availability, convenience, and physical requirements. As leisure time increases, allow for more time to cultivate choices, to branch out and explore new interests. Who says you have to do only one thing when you retire? In retirement, you will have roughly fifty extra hours a week to do all the things you have always wanted to do but never had time for before.

How Will You Spend Your Time?

FUN

One goal of a balanced program of leisure activities is to provide *fun*. The single person has the advantage of making individual choices and the freedom to engage in activities alone or with others.

Fun Activities	Where Available	Participation: Alone or with Company	Approximate Cost
1.			
2.			
3.			
4.			

A LEISURELY THOUGHT:
I've taken my fun where I've found it.
—RUDYARD KIPLING

How Will You Spend Your Time?

NEW FRIENDS

One goal of a balanced program of leisure activities is to provide new social relationships with *new friends*. Taking the initiative and inviting others to join in can be the beginning of companionship for single people.

The WHYS of Making New Friends	Where to Make Friends	Going Alone or with Company	Expenses Involved
1.			
2.			
3.			
4.			

A LEISURELY THOUGHT:
The best rule of friendship is to keep your heart a little softer than your head.
—GEORGE SANTAYANA

LEISURE FOR A LIFETIME

How Will You Spend Your Time?

EXPOSURE TO NEW IDEAS

One goal of a balanced program of leisure activities is to provide exposure to *new, challenging ideas*.

Activities for Exposure to New Ideas	Where Available	Participation: Alone or with Company	Expenses Involved
1.			
2.			
3.			
4.			

A LEISURELY THOUGHT:
If people who do not understand each other at least understand that they do not understand each other, then they understand each other better than when, not understanding each other, they do not even understand that they do not understand each other.
—GUSTAV ISCHHEISER:
APPEARANCES AND REALITIES

How Will You Spend Your Time?

COMMUNITY SERVICE

One goal of a balanced program of leisure activities is to provide *opportunities for volunteer work*. A commitment of time can provide structure, recognition, and status for single men and women.

Community Service and Volunteer Work of Interest	Location	Participation: Alone or with Associates	Expenses Involved
1.			
2.			
3.			
4.			

A LEISURELY THOUGHT:
Wherever a man turns, he can find someone who needs him. Even if it is a little thing, do something for which you get no pay but the privilege of doing it. For remember, you don't live in a world all your own. Your brothers are here, too.
—DR. ALBERT SCHWEITZER

LEISURE FOR A LIFETIME

How Will You Spend Your Time?

EXERCISE

One goal of a balanced program of leisure activities is to provide a *balanced program of exercise.* This gives you an excellent way to socialize, to let off steam, and to live a healthier life.

Exercise Activity of Interest	Location	Participation: Alone or with Companions	Estimated Expenses
1.			
2.			
3.			
4.			

A LEISURELY THOUGHT:
All animals except man know that the chief business of life is to enjoy it.
—SAMUEL BUTLER

Putting Leisure Choices into Action

With all the new ideas you have, let's block out an exciting series of leisure experiences for now and days ahead. This will make for a happier and smoother transition from midlife into retirement. Block in below your choice of leisure activity for a minimum of one hour for each day of the week. Put your plan into action today.

Day	Hours Involved	Activity	Special Features
SUNDAY			
MONDAY			
TUESDAY			
WEDNESDAY			
THURSDAY			

FRIDAY			
SATURDAY			

Note:
Chart yourself a *monthly* leisure plan, too. Observe how leisure plans are affected by seasonal changes and holiday changes.

A LEISURELY THOUGHT:
One ought, every day at least, to hear a little song, read a good poem, see a fine picture, and, if it were possible, to speak a few reasonable words.
—JOHANN W. VON GOETHE

5
Solo Traveling

General Words of Advice

Where do I go to find out what opportunities exist for me as a solo traveler?

It is amazing how many choices are available to mature singles wishing to travel. Agencies catering to single travelers have multiplied throughout the United States. State tourist bureaus will supply you with valuable travel brochures and provide helpful information about accommodations should you decide to venture cross country. They can tune you in to other possibilities as well. Some retirees choose to sublet quarters in other states for weeks or even months, preferring to "settle" in one place rather than continually move around. Possibilities are endless once you give in to your sense of adventure and begin exploring where and how you prefer to travel. Do your homework now, when time is on your side. Read. Speak to travel agents. Send for travel material from alumni associations and/or fraternal and professional groups to which you belong. Refer to organizations for retired people and to religious groups. Or just plain talk over possibilities with other middle-agers, whether married or single.

Solo Traveling

You are bound to discover a wealth of new ideas, and the planning can be as much fun as the actual traveling.

What do I do about the problems that arise when traveling solo?

A well-informed travel adviser recommends in particular that single travelers learn to speak up and assert themselves. That will result in their realizing many of their needs. People are basically friendly everywhere and ready to help once they know what you want or need. She doesn't think singles need be afraid to travel alone.

On a specific level, she recommends paying the single supplement, if you can afford to, in order to be able to cater to yourself at the close of a busy travel day. On the other hand, she suggests that single travelers advise the booking person before departing on a trip or reserving space if they want to share a room. That way you may learn in advance of others desiring to share, and be able to screen your potential travel roommate to ascertain mutual compatibility when it comes to things like smoking, partying, snoring, and other habits. Sharing accommodations with a stranger can sometimes be a problem for the single traveler. You will have to decide if it is worth the saving in room fees.

On a group trip to Los Angeles, there was only one accommodation left, and that required Rita's sharing a room with another single. She had no opportunity to prescreen, and her roommate turned out to be an energetic twenty-two-year-old woman who loved partying and late hours. Since the hotel management provided only one room key, which they were required to share, Rita spent her sleeping hours half-awake, listening for her roommate's knock on the door.

On another trip, Rita made her decision to share in advance. But there is always the unpredictable to contend with. Her partner developed a cold, and the wheezing and sneezing made both uncomfortable.

In the final analysis, you will have to determine whether paying a single supplement, which can sometimes be steep, or sharing a room, which is sometimes uncomfortable, is the best solution.

Are there solutions to this kind of travel pitfall for the mature single?

In Rita's case, no amount of assertion with either the hotel management or with the tour leaders resulted in a room change. But Rita at least had the satisfaction of making her discomfort known. She couldn't fault herself for having to put up with that. Now she knows that it's better to take a single room wherever possible.

Whenever you get poor service at the cost of reasonable service, as when you find yourself shoehorned into the former maid's room in a hotel where you have paid the supplement, speak up and ask for a change. You do not have to accept inconsiderate treatment just because you are traveling alone. You certainly won't get better treatment by keeping silent. You may well succeed in improving your situation. If that move is impossible, accept the situation as long as you have to and concentrate instead on having as good a time as you can.

Foreign Travel Options

What about traveling out of the country by yourself? It's easy to imagine meeting people and coping by yourself in this country, but going it alone in a foreign country doesn't sound like much fun to me.

It's not, unless you love isolation. But there is no reason why the midlife single has to travel alone. Join a tour group and travel abroad with others, married or single. College alumni associations and many museums offer special interest tours. You might enjoy a tour group organized to pursue a common interest, such as archeology. Commercial travel services such as International Weekends Charter Vacations, Inc., of 1170 Commonwealth Avenue, Boston, Massachusetts 02134, offer one and two week inexpensive, quality packages abroad, as does Carefree David of 955 N.E. 125 Street, North Miami, Florida 33161. Some tours, for example, those offered by AARP, 215 Long Beach Boulevard, Long Beach, California 90801, are specifically for men and women in their later years. If you prefer to travel with single men and women only, ask your travel agent to recommend such a travel group.

The advantage of traveling with a tour is that there are people options present. In other words, if you want company while sightseeing, for meals, or for exploring the night life, it is available. You also generally have the option of keeping to yourself if you wish. The point is, you have a choice!

Consult associations you belong to, and add your name to their travel mailing list. Speak to a travel agent and ask him or her to alert you to interesting tours. And become a persistent reader of the travel page or section of your newspaper. Purchase a travel magazine or two. Exchange ideas with seasoned travelers.

I'm too independent to be led around by a tour leader. I've been alone all my life, and my idea of fun when traveling is to do what I want and stop where I want.

To some people, that challenge is fun. The pleasure of flying to London and taking off on a day's journey to Stonehenge excites them. Discovering unique places, such as the fado centers of Portugal, delights them. Driving down an Old World country road and pulling off to the side to enjoy a magnificent sunset fulfills them.

Bettina, a divorcee, still talks about the delightful trip she made alone to Copenhagen. She spent the first night in a reserved hotel room, then headed for the railroad station the following morning. A room reservation office there was set up to help travelers find accommodations in private homes. For three nights, and at an unbelievably low rate, she boarded in the home of a concert pianist, just a ten-minute ride from downtown Copenhagen. Since she would be in Scandinavia three weeks and planned to fly home out of Copenhagen, she arranged to leave her excess baggage with her landlady while she traveled around Denmark, Sweden, and Norway. The railroad pass she purchased in Copenhagen permitted her to stop and board where and when she pleased in Denmark and Sweden. Room accommodations, pleasant and comfortable, were available in different cities through railroad bureaus and local chambers of commerce, where invariably someone spoke English. She roomed in different private homes, in teachers' quarters, in student dormitories, and in small hotels. She found each place comfortable, clean, and attractive. In Norway, she was required to purchase an additional pass, which provided travel privileges on the railroads, the buses of the mountain regions, and the steamers that sailed the fjords. She was traveling on a limited budget, so she took her breakfasts in the local bakeries, lunched on park benches, and had dinner in a comfortable family-style restaurant. She took delight in her own resourcefulness during a wonderful trip and to this day retains an inner glow thinking of the people she met, the adventures she shared, and the fun she had.

People who know what they would enjoy are ahead of the game. But suppose you are like me, alone, middle-aged, and close to retirement, but ignorant of what would provide the most enjoyment in traveling abroad. What would you do?

Make a real effort to find out what would interest me most in travel abroad. Perhaps you would prefer to spend a week exploring a country or city where the language is familiar. How about England, or just London? That would make your first trip abroad easy. Maybe you have a special interest you could pursue in another country. For example, if Renaissance art delights you, think about a visit to Florence or Rome. Take time to visit the library, or buy some travel books to learn about different countries. Investigate economical travel possibilities. A good travel agent can be a real help.

I am way past the travel agent stage as far as advice on where to go is concerned. I'm single and retired, and I have already done a good deal of traveling. When I go abroad, I always travel with a single male companion. We give parties in the hotel we stay in. Everybody has a lot of fun.

Singles who travel with a friend rarely complain of loneliness. And if they are sociable, they can choose to entertain others, too. Ben did this when he was in Nice, France. He met a group of Frenchmen on the beach and invited them to a party in his room. It was a safe thing to do because there were security officers in the hotel. In return, he was invited to local social gatherings during his week in Nice.

Of course, if you do not have a travel companion, you should be cautious in extending or accepting invitations. A night-life tour with reliable escorts provided by a local tour company could provide an alternative. Some solo travelers enjoy a quiet evening, sipping a glass of wine in a local bistro. Dorothy, who is widowed, did this and had a good time watching the passing parade in Tel Aviv, Israel.

Some singles plan an evening trip to a local casino. Fred, a retired man who has always been single, enjoyed evenings at casinos in London, Ostend, and Monte Carlo. In each case, he made arrangements through the hotel concierge for a night tour bus to pick him up at his hotel, to drop him at the casino, and to return him to his hotel. The tour was inexpensive, and Fred protected himself from losing too much money by setting a limit on the amount he would gamble. When this sum was exhausted, Fred watched others play blackjack or roulette until the tour bus was ready to return him to his hotel.

My network of acquaintances has dwindled. Since my wife died three years ago, I bury myself in work. I've forgotten how to play. Maybe I should revive the interest we shared in traveling abroad.

Everyone needs a change of pace, and renewing yourself by doing something to break the daily routine can recharge your internal battery. Take a lesson from Harry, a widower with a demanding law practice, who loved to travel abroad when his wife was alive. One of their favorite places was Saint Maarten. They enjoyed the warm weather, the beaches, and light gambling at the casino. Now Harry travels with a male friend. While it is a different type of travel than that he enjoyed with his late wife, he knows he must balance the pressures of his work with leisurely fun in order to preserve his physical and psychological health. Adaptability during the work years prepares people for the adjustments retirement requires, too.

It's Friendship, Friendship

Traveling together can strengthen or weaken the friendship between women alone. I'm willing to risk it because it's preferable to going abroad alone or with strangers in a group.

Testing the waters is one way of determining what suits you. It not only permits you to evaluate options, but affords you the opportunity to make choices and changes based upon what you have learned. If the trip abroad strengthens the friendship between you and a travel companion, wonderful! If not, your next trip abroad can be structured in a different way.

Consider taking a short trip first with someone you see as a potential companion for travel abroad or extended vacations in this country. You'll get a good idea of whether travel will deepen the closeness between you. If it does, you'll be more confident about making further travel plans together. You will find yourself blessed with a compatible travel companion.

Sometimes, of course, you'll be ready to risk a longer trip right away. Leila, a widow, worried about too much time on her hands, about eating alone, and about feeling lonely and lost if she traveled without company. She made friends with Kate, a divorcee. After a short acquaintance, they decided to travel together to the Canary Islands as members of a larger group. There were adjustments and compromises each found she had to make, but they enjoyed each other's company and came home better friends than when they left.

Traveling abroad often provides opportunities to make new friends who enhance the enjoyment of leisure, right?

Right. People love to do things together. That is why the loss of a mate can be so devastating. It's natural for

Solo Traveling

men and women to search for new companions to replace the loss.

In a balanced leisure program, you have time with and for others and space for yourself. But to enjoy your leisure, it is essential you use your time meaningfully. Sometimes you will want to participate in events with others in order to share your pleasures. As an aware mature single, whether working or retired, you can use leisure hours to make new friends. When you meet people you like, feel free to extend social invitations. Hand out your card, or exchange telephone numbers.

Sadie, a divorcee aboard a Florida-bound plane, found herself seated next to Jane, also divorced. Jane was bound for Paradise Island. As the two ladies conversed, they discovered they had mutual interests. A few weeks later, after both returned home, Jane phoned Sadie. They met for dinner, and a new friendship sprouted. Since both liked to travel, they are now discussing a possible future trip abroad together.

I know of similar instances where people traveling alone made lifelong friends because they were receptive to opportunities.

It does not happen just in the movies or television! It is possible to cite case after case of singles making friends because they opened up. For example, Elise, a middle-aged divorcee, was traveling in Finland with a small tour group of Americans. She had more in common with a couple, a physician and his wife, than with the two other single ladies on the tour. Together with the couple, Elise rented a taxi and guide to travel to small outlying towns. Their friendship continued long after the tour returned to the United States, and to this day, Elise's life is enriched by knowing this couple.

Stephanie, a widow traveling in Jamaica with her teen-aged children, had a comparable experience. One evening at dinner in their hotel, the children started a conversation with the middle-aged couple seated next to them. It was the couple's second marriage and they were in Jamaica on their honeymoon. They missed their children, who were home in England, so when Stephanie's children opened the conversation, they were receptive. Later, the couple invited Stephanie to be their guests in the hotel nightclub. After Stephanie and her children returned to the United States she corresponded with their new English friends. Several years later, the English family, children included, visited Stephanie. And when she later visited England, Stephanie stayed at their home in the Midlands.

So you see, it is possible to make friends traveling abroad. You can make them through planning a strategy—going with tour groups where you meet people with similar interests, through activities, through other people, or just naturally by chance. Then, when you retire, you can use those extra hours of leisure to visit your national and international friends, and to have them visit you.

I don't have time to invest in making friends abroad. I'm a recently separated man close to retirement. I'm hoping

Solo Traveling

to fly El-Al for a two-week trip to Israel, and there is much I want to see and do there. I don't have to have people to be with. So I'm planning to go from sightseeing to sleep.

There is no one formula to suit every mature single traveling at home or abroad. If you have found a way of traveling that suits you, that is all that matters.

I meet older men who are single and have never traveled abroad. All they know is work. What will they do in their retired years if they do not know how to make friends or have never been more than one hundred miles away from their home town?

They will do with their leisure what they are capable of doing, and in their own way. Perhaps they will rise to the challenge of their new retired lives.

Bernie, divorced, retired from the garage business and made his first trip at the mature age of fifty-five. Prior to that, his only travel abroad had been in World War II. While he often spoke of traveling, he never quite got to it. His first pleasure trip abroad was a cruise to St. Thomas in the Virgin Islands and to Puerto Rico. Bernie had shortly before become acquainted with a new group of men and women. They all belonged to a singles' club. When this club announced the cruise, Bernie decided to get up and go!

There are many agencies providing opportunities for travel abroad. Singles' associations regularly offer trips and sometimes supply roommates to save your paying the single supplement. Some of them arrange for meetings with local singles groups, thereby providing travelers with opportunities to make new friends all over the world.

I don't need such a service. I've met many singles since my divorce, and I've been spreading the good word about overseas' organizations that help their countrymen and women meet travelers from other countries.

Sweden has such a program, called Sweden at Home. It enables you to spend an afternoon or evening in an English-speaking Swedish home with Swedes of similar interests and background. It takes about two days to arrange a meeting. If you plan to be in Stockholm for a few days, go to Sweden House, Hamngatan 27, and introduce yourself.

Hilda, a schoolteacher who has always been single, found a similar program in Amsterdam, Holland, and was matched with a schoolteacher living there. Not only did Hilda enjoy the home visit, she was also escorted to the Zuider Zee by the Dutch schoolteacher, and she had the opportunity to make other side trips with her new friend.

Before you depart on your journey abroad, write to the appropriate foreign consulate, embassy, or tourist bureau for the name of an agency that arranges visits to native homes. Not every country has such a program, but those that do provide you with a wonderful opportunity.

After thirty years of marriage, which recently ended in divorce, I am seeking roots. I won't find them in programs featuring visits to strangers of similar background and inter-

ests. I want to visit my family abroad whose friendship I need now.

Marvin traveled to Argentina for the same reason. As holiday time approached, he felt particularly lonely. He wrote to Argentina and his family there invited him to their home. He left the December cold of the Northeast for a family reunion and holiday with friends in Argentina, where the weather and the people gave him a warm welcome.

There are other ways of making connections with people when you travel abroad. You can travel to follow up on interests and hobbies you have.

Precisely! Many people have a passion for something or other. They can often pursue their particular interests wherever they go, even overcoming a language barrier. For example, if you have a love for bridge, as Phil, a widower, did, you can find a bridge club almost anywhere. Ask for information from your hotel concierge or the local tourist bureau, or simply look through the telephone directory. Phil found clubs in Geneva, Switzerland, in Nice and Evian, France, and in London, England. Arthur had a passion for tennis and found a tennis club or tennis court wherever he traveled. Terry, a divorcee, loved to swim and through the hotel concierge in Lima, Peru, located the name of the international beach club in that city. She also discovered the location of the Hebraic Swim Club outside Lima. At both clubs she met Latin Americans from Brazil and Argentina as well as Peruvians. She even met a Peruvian who volunteered the services of his mother to take Terry shopping in Lima. Each of these Americans was invited to the homes of native Swiss, Frenchmen, and Peruvians.

I'm pleased to learn of so many different ways that singles have made friends.

Let us add one more illustration. Ingrid, a retired schoolteacher and a widow, contacted a Swiss teachers' organization in order to rent an apartment in Lausanne one summer. She lived abroad for six weeks and sublet a Swiss teacher's apartment. She made many Swiss friends that summer.

Let me make another suggestion. You can make friends abroad by exchanging homes and apartments in the United States and abroad.

This is possible through advertisements in international newspapers. But a safer, more efficient way to do this is through the Vacation Exchange Club (address: 350 Broadway, New York, New York 10013), an organization that is in the business of listing places for exchanges abroad and in Hawaii and Alaska. Also, send to Gum Publications, 3535 Ross Ave., Suite 307, San Jose, California 95124, for "Your Place and Mine: A Guide to Vacation Home Exchange." This booklet defines responsibilities, advises you how to negotiate an exchange, and instructs you what to do if an exchange proves a problem. Both the Vacation Exchange Club and Gum Publications charge you for their services. But what better investment can you make if you are considering spending a good deal of your retired life traveling abroad? Exchanging homes or apartments can build international friendships.

Approved Exposure—to New Ideas

Different civilizations intrigue me. I've always been curious about how people built their worlds. My first trip abroad, which was with a tour, was to Israel, where I was exposed to civilization upon civilization.

Opportunities for enrichment through travel are tremendous. Colleges are offering study programs, both credit and noncredit, for mature adults. There are escorted programs in China, France, Ireland and England, Greece, West Africa, the Galapagos Islands, and Italy. Write to the International Studies Department, University of California Extension, 2223 Fulton St., Berkeley, California 94720, about opportunities to study Chaucer in Canterbury; Egyptian history at sites along the Nile; Indian art, architecture, and religion in Bombay, Delhi, Benares, Madras, and Katmandu; or Renaissance art in Florence and Sienna. For the independent soul, the International Programs Division, Western Illinois University, Macomb, Illinois 61455 in the midwest invites the travelers to make their own travel plans, to meet the coordinating professor for an individual conference, and to combine travel with study. Academic credit is available from twenty different study units.

I'm one for exposing myself to new ideas, but I want a lighter program of travel abroad. Life has been hard and money is tight. I want my widowed years to be more carefree.

Then Elderhostel would be suitable for you. In this program you live on a college campus. The fees are nominal and the courses interesting. For example, past programs on Canadian campuses have included gold panning at Keyano College, Alberta; Canada Today at Brandon University in Manitoba; Songs and Stories in Newfoundland at Memorial University of Newfoundland; or the Supply of Money at Carleton University in Ontario. You must be sixty years of age to enroll in Elderhostel, and the wonderful thing for singles is that you will be with stimulating people.

Another interesting concept in travel is engaging in your own study tour of a subject that interests you. For example, make your own itinerary of the gardens of Britain, Spain, France, and Italy. You can compare concepts in landscaping as well as savor the beauty of the area. Or, if you are Orient-bound, you could tour the rock gardens of Japan.

That's exactly what I intend to do. Since I have been single all of my life, I have used leisure time to cultivate my love for ballet. I'm Venice-bound this summer to combine a vacation with the international ballet festival there. When I retire, I intend to do more of this.

People who combine interests with travel have a direction. Sometimes retired film devotees choose to attend the film festival in Cannes, France. Other retirees study French in Villefrance-sur-Mer in France or participate in theater programs in Oxford, England or learn weaving in Helsinki, Finland. Knowing the direction to take in pursuit of their interests, they utilize time meaningfully and economically.

Even if you haven't yet developed special interests, you can still enjoy travel abroad. I took an inexpensive cruise to the Caribbean, and participated in many activities I found worthwhile.

Ingrid, a divorcee in her middle years, took a cruise to the West Indies. She, too, traveled on an economy rate. All day long there were lectures to attend, finance talks, classes in bridge and arts and crafts, and instruction in golf. After class, conversation flowed. In addition, the liner stopped at two different Caribbean ports, and she had the opportunity to see how others lived, to sample different foods, and to try out a different language. The cruise made Ingrid's world wider and more interesting.

So in part what you are saying is that single people can discover what interests them through travel abroad, sometimes accidentally.

Yes, and once you make that discovery, capitalize upon it. Mervin, a man who has always been single, became enchanted with the sound of Italian on a visit to Italy. He continued studying the language, enrolling in a course in an Italian institute back home. Jill, a divorcee, worked in Geneva, Switzerland, for eight weeks. There she renewed her knowledge of French, which she had last spoken in high school more than thirty years before. Determined not to lose this renewed pleasure, Jill took an adult high school course in French when she returned to the United States. She was not aiming for a diploma or course credit. She simply wanted to learn to speak French more fluently.

Volunteers, Front and Center!

I'm planning to retire to Israel in a few years. Even though I am alone, I consider myself fortunate because my health is good and my finances adequate. I'd like to say "thank you" by doing volunteer work for part of my leisure hours and put my teaching experience to active use.

The feeling of well-being that results from giving to others is very special, and certainly retirees can put leisure time to important use doing volunteer work abroad. An organization called Teachers on Volunteer Service in Israel is calling for volunteers to tutor Israelis in English. Information about the program is available from TOVS, Department of Education and Culture, 515 Park Avenue, New York, New York 10022. For information about other countries and volunteer work you can do, write to the consulate for the country of your interest. There are foreign consulates in many major cities, or you can write to the consular division of the country's embassy in Washington, D.C. Your letter will be forwarded to the appropriate source.

I'm happy to see opportunities for volunteer work with organizations other than health-related groups. I know how much hospitals need help, but I couldn't give to a hospital now, particularly since I've been in and out of hospitals for years, ever since my wife became ill. Now that I'm alone, I want healthier worlds.

If you are planning to live abroad for an extended period or to retire abroad and you wish to do volunteer work, there are English-speaking schools that need help. Sometimes relief organizations welcome the help of Americans. There are also bilingual organizations that welcome English-speaking volunteers. In most major cities abroad, there are English-speaking clubs. Contact them when you settle in, and see what the leadership would suggest. Naturally, the offerings will not be as numerous as at home, where you could choose from many groups. But there are worthwhile agencies that will welcome your volunteer services.

One side benefit of volunteering, if you live abroad, is making friends in the organization. I don't want to be isolated when I retire to Italy. I recently separated from my husband, and I'm seeking to establish new roots.

By volunteering, you will be doing good for others and for yourself. This is particularly valuable for mature singles, because it is a way of moving away from yourself and thinking of others. By focusing on what others need, you take away some of the self-imposed stress that aloneness produces in many people, widowed, divorced, or separated. And, as you say, opportunities to make new friends are present in volunteer organizations—friends who like you and are sharing and helping.

Bend and Stretch: Un, Deux, Trois, Quatre

As a golfer, I like to spend time on the golf courses when I travel abroad. As a single near retirement, I'm figuring on golfing a good deal more in the years to come and combining it with travel.

Travel agencies and airlines are featuring more travel packages than ever built around enjoying a sport. Many of them offer golfers opportunities to golf in Scotland or Canada or on courses in other parts of the world. Your travel agent is a source of information for sports travel. Often sports magazines advertise trips abroad based upon a sports interest.

Florence, a divorcee, makes golf the center of her trips abroad. She has golfed in Nova Scotia, in Ireland, and in Spain. Even where the language is foreign, Florence maintains she rarely has a problem around the golf course. It seems there is a language common to any special interest that overcomes any linguistic problem. Florence enjoys the differences and international flavor, the opportunity to meet new people with similar interests, and the chance to have fun playing golf abroad.

That's half the battle, having fun in your leisure hours. I, too, love to travel abroad, and my tennis racket is always my worthwhile companion. I find a few hours of tennis a day most fulfilling.

Precisely. You can make tennis your fill-in activity, or you can travel with a tennis group, combining tennis and travel abroad. Either way you have opportunities to release tension, to have fun, to learn about the people and cultures of other countries, in short, to expand your world.

Whenever Sidney, a middle-aged widower, travels, he learns from the hotel concierge where the tennis courts are. He inquires how to arrange games. To date he has played tennis in Switzerland, France, Spain, and Ecuador. Sometimes there are courts at the hotel where he is staying; sometimes he locates public courts; sometimes the tennis courts are available at private clubs that permit him to use their facilities for a fee.

It is possible to learn the location of tennis facilities for your trip abroad from the tourist bureau or the consulate in Washington, D.C., for your country of interest. That way you have the information you want in English already before you leave.

Concierges are knowledgeable and therefore useful people. Even though I am alone, my life is busy, and I don't always have time to preplan a trip thoroughly. I live by the credo "Ask the concierge."

Good advice. The concierge is especially important to a traveler alone.

Greta, an always single middle-aged woman with a love for swimming, inquired of the hotel concierge about the private swim clubs of Mexico City when she visited there. He directed her to an international swim club where, for a modest fee, she was able to swim as a guest for the day. The idea is to use your creativity to give yourself a good time.

And, while you are at it, let others do the exercise and you do the observing. That can be fun, too.

Yes, indeed.

Roslyn, a middle-aged divorcee, loved to go to the race track from time to time. When she visited Lima, Peru, she organized a group within her larger group to spend an evening at the races. Not only did she meet horse breeders who spoke English, but she enjoyed the beauty of the track, including the magnificent landscaping and flower beds. She says that the few pesos she lost betting on the races was minor compared to the pleasure of her visit.

If you are visiting Mexico City, you may want to attend the jai-alai games.

With all this exercise, should the middle-aged traveler or older man or woman be prepared for health emergencies? What happens if you pull a muscle or wrench your back?

It is wise to prepare to safeguard your health abroad. Many doctors recommend you double the amount of medicine you expect to need, in case you cannot duplicate it abroad. Bring copies of your prescriptions. If flying from city to city abroad, carry medical supplies as hand baggage so they arrive with you and not in another city. Sometimes brand names of medicines are different in foreign countries, so if you are planning a trip abroad, ask your doctor for the generic names.

Membership is free in the International Association for Medical Assistance to Travelers, which makes available a directory of clinics, hospitals, and English-speaking doctors worldwide. However, a donation is welcome. Write to this organization at 123 Edward Street, Suite 725, Toronto, Canada M5G 1E2. Then, if you fall off a horse, as Zane did when he traveled alone to Portugal, you will know where to obtain the services of an English-speaking physician, whose fees are fixed by the International Association for Medical Assistance to Travelers. That should make you feel more protected.

I'm ready to go. As a single making my first trip abroad alone, I'll start small and grow tall.
    Limber up. Then stretch your horizons gradually.

6
Work Is Just a Four=Letter Word

"Work" Versus Work

I always thought retirement meant the end of work, but here I am, thinking of continuing in some kind of work when I retire.

Look around you, and you will see a wide-open retirement world. Some people are fully retired. Others have returned to part-time work. They are checking with Social Security about the maximum they can earn in retirement without forfeiting benefits. Despite the cost-of-living hikes built into Social Security and into some pension plans, inflation has taken a chunk off retirement income. By working part-time, many retirees find they can make ends meet more easily and continue living in the life-style they are accustomed to. Today many middle-aged singles engaged in full-time employment are already using free time to explore retirement work opportunities.

Continuing to work can also compensate for changes in structure retirement brings. I know many singles who are upset about the loss of the nine to five routine.

The set routine of getting up to go to work and coming home a certain time is something many single retirees miss. An alternate routine is the compensating attraction of part-time work. Then, too, longer life expectancies motivate other singles to work part-time in retirement. Many people grow weary of full-time leisure.

While it is harder for older people to find employment than for younger workers, their skills are valuable to many companies in training younger employees. Sometimes older workers are invited to remain as consultants. A recent study in a national magazine reported predictions by experts that, except for recession-hit industries, more older workers will be needed to fill employment gaps in coming years. The thing to do is get ready before retirement by exploring future work opportunities now.

Let's hear more about the mature labor market.

Already one-third of the people over sixty-five are employed in part-time jobs, which are less demanding and more plentiful than full-time positions in many areas. The Wall Street Journal in New York City quoted fast food chains as saying that more and more older workers will appear behind counters in years to come. Mature workers are valued for promptness and productivity, giving a full day's work for a full day's pay—or, in retired language, a part-time day's work for a part-time day's pay.

Do many retired people find work?

A 1981 report from the U.S. Labor Department stated that 20 percent of all Americans who retire return to work, at least part-time. A major study of the retirement patterns of white male workers found that the likelihood of full retirement increases sharply with age, rising from 10 percent for those aged fifty-eight to sixty-one, to about 70 percent for those aged sixty-five to sixty-nine. Individuals, aged sixty-five to sixty-nine are almost as likely to be partially retired as they are to be working full-time. Of the sixty-six-year-olds working part-time, 28 percent earn a wage that is at least 40 percent lower than that earned in their preretirement job. Thirty percent have remained at their old job, but work fewer hours, with no wage reduction. And 42 percent experience a 40 percent cut in both hours and wages. A typical worker who is sixty-three and not covered by a pension has only an 11 percent probability of retiring completely. A pensioned worker of the same age has a 27 percent probability of retiring completely. Maybe some of this information could be useful in planning your own solo retirement.

What Can I Do?

Single friends who have retired tell me of the long hours alone. But if I were to work, I would want a change of employment. The trouble is I don't know what else I'm qualified for.

You have two basic choices: working for yourself or

working for others. To point yourself in the right direction, use the inventory at the close of this chapter, or make your own list of possible occupations.

I don't need to take inventory to know that at this stage of life I would be cautious about going into my own business venture. Where are the jobs working for others?

Most of the jobs are in service industries. Schools, movie theaters, department stores, and catering firms offer part-time employment. Marketability increases if you are available to work hours others avoid. Evening employment could provide an interesting break in long retired days. Shopping centers, doctors, dentists, hotels, and motels hire older evening workers. Security work, as a watchman or guard, is possible, too. When summer approaches, banks, department stores, and offices hire people to replace vacationing staff. Often a temporary job can open opportunities for employment at other times of the year.

If you are planning to live in a retirement area, you will find jobs plentiful. Notice the faces behind retail counters. They are faces of retirees resettled in the community.

If you need still more convincing of the growing popularity of the mature worker, take heed of a study conducted by William M. Mercer, benefits consultants. Nearly 90 percent of employers believe that older workers are more committed to company objectives than their younger counterparts. This was determined by polling 552 chief executives, of which 76 percent said they would more likely hire someone over age fifty than under because older workers perform better. So it looks as if the job market for retirees has extended into the corporate world.

How do I find out about job opportunities?
There are several suggestions for you to consider.

Contact employment agencies specializing in placing older workers. Many of them place newspaper ads specifically addressed to mature readers. If no such ads appear in your newspaper, telephone one or two major agencies and ask if they place mature workers. Scan want ads. *The New York Times* carried an ad for retirees to counsel women planning their own businesses.

Utilize your free time as a single to explore job opportunities. Browse through the Yellow Pages for employment ideas. This may help direct you to where and how you could be employed. Telephone the personnel official for an interview with a company that interests you.

Inquire at your union office, the United States Civil Service Office, professional associations, and state and federal job training and employment services about the mature job market. Look through industrial directories. Contact the Forty-Plus Clubs for executives. If you have had military service, write to the Retired Officers Association at 201 North Washington Street, Alexandria, Virginia 22314.

The business section of my local newspaper has turned out to be a good source of future employment information. Even though the jobs listed are for full-time employment, I find I can pinpoint job directions.

Companies often advertise in business sections of newspapers for people with financial, engineering, computer, sales, or business backgrounds. You could get an idea of where your experience might fit in. Think about contacting advertisers to inquire about part-time employment in your area of specialty. Ingenuity pays off.

My plan is to follow job trends as indicated by newly established college curriculums.

It is possible to see where future jobs will be by viewing new college programs. One college in the Northeast is offering new graduate certificates in travel, gerontology, fund raising, and health management. You can bet these are growing job markets, because colleges attract enrollees with the promise of preparation for future employment. In order for a new curriculum to be offered, it must be developed, then approved by faculty committees and the administration. All of this takes research and time. Therefore, once a new program is offered, you can reasonably assume a job trend in that direction. Why not use your single middle years to read the education page of your newspaper and to send for college catalogs?

What about possibilities in one's own company?

Many companies are hiring their own retirees—as consultants, on a part-time basis to train newcomers, and also to fill in for vacationing staff. So be certain to register with your own personnel department. Remember, too, that singles are premium employees because of their ready availability and freedom to commit themselves as replacement personnel, consultants, advisers, or trainers.

Find out if your company offers up-front dollars to older employees who wish to go to school to prepare themselves for postretirement careers. One major national company offers $2500 in preretirement tuition for college courses providing job training.

My town recently featured a job fair for older workers. The local TV station brought together mature people and employers to publicize job opportunities. It was a huge success.

Other television stations are undertaking similar projects. For example, a local television station, together with state, county, and local organizations for the aging in New York and New Jersey, brought together older people seeking employment and corporations open to employing older workers. It was a showcase of opportunities and ten thousand job seekers turned out for this job fair. It's important to keep alert to the many possibilities around.

Who's the Boss?

I will certainly put many of my single hours to work in my retired years. Let's talk some more about the choices between working for myself or working for others.

One way of making the choice is to establish what you enjoy doing with your time. Do you, for instance, have a flair for any of the following: crafts, cooking, machine maintenance or repair, carpentry, teaching, writing, sewing, drawing, or commercial services? Tom, a salesman for a major foods organization, intends to set up his own diesel engine repair shop when he retires. He's a pro at mechanics, loves tinkering, and he wants a change from sales. Most of all, he wants to be his own boss. Beth, a widow, has always been interested in nutrition, and she has a flair for the dramatic. She's planning to spend her mature years lecturing about nutrition for a major health organization. Once you determine what you wish to do, the decision whether to pursue it independently or work for another will come naturally.

I have no problem making this decision. I always wanted to be in my own business but never wanted to risk it while I had a family to support. Now that I'm a widower and my children are grown, I plan to use some money to open a small carpentry business. Where can I go for practical advice?

The United States Small Business Administration offers advice on starting a business. They offer seminars and courses. You can obtain individual counseling from SBA's Senior Corps of Retired Executives (SCORE) and the Active Corps of Executives (AGE). If there is no regional SBA office listed in your telephone directory, write to the national office: the United States Small Business Administration, Washington, D.C. 20416.

Another source for guidance in starting up your own business is your local chamber of commerce.

Women, if there is a branch of Women Business

Owners in your area, take advantage of their programs in marketing, finance, sales, publicity, time management, and organization. Most important of all, use free hours in your middle years to scout around for help in starting your own business. Solicit advice from successful people currently owning their own businesses.

Are there advantages to owning your own business? Do they outweigh the disadvantages?

Let me answer this with an illustration. Sandra, a widow, was offered the rare choice of buying into a business in which she had been an employee for years, or of continuing to work for her employers. She explored her options carefully, even attended meetings of local business associations in order to make an educated choice. This is what she discovered:

The advantage of working for others is that no outlay of capital is necessary, so there is no dollar risk. The hours are defined. Social contacts are easy to establish. The disadvantage of working for others is that income is limited to what you are paid. Opportunities for creativity may not be present, and so you risk boredom.

The advantage of being in your own business is the freedom to make decisions for yourself, rather than have someone else do it for you. There is also the possibility of good income with or without Social Security. The disadvantage of being in your own business is that it often ties you down. Another disadvantage is that you are more susceptible to outside factors that can affect the business, such as security problems or problems in the economy.

Work Is Just a Four-Letter Word 149

Could you present a capsule view of where the jobs are for mature workers? I think this is my leaning, rather than being tied down in my own business.

Think in terms of three basic categories: service industries, general business firms, and community services.

Service industries include real estate companies, confectionery shops, restaurants and catering shops, churches, travel agencies, health care institutions, schools, libraries, banks, retail stores, and movie theaters.

In the second category, general business firms, you could work as a consultant, a trainer of younger employees, or as an administrator or employee for temporary duty in any of these corporate areas: management, finance, fund-raising, promotion, sales, customer service, business development and acquisition. Business fields open include anything from manufacturing to nonprofit organizations, retailing, communications, and the arts.

In the third category, you could apply for a community service position in transportation, tutoring, home health care, recreation, or any service the community offers.

Applying: It's Been a Long, Long Time

Since I was widowed, three years ago, I just don't know what to do with myself. Fortunately, my husband left me in good financial shape and I don't have to work nor did I have to work while he was alive. Volunteer work does not appeal to me. I'd like to find a small paying job. I'm told I need a resumé. What do I put in it?

Define and describe what you have done in your adult lifetime. Anything that indicates leadership, responsibility, and skills is top priority. It's not just a matter of jobs held. What community or church group have you been active in? What volunteer work have you done? Be honest in describing yourself. The resumé is an important tool for entry or reentry into the job market, and your resumé could open doors. If you have the money for it, why not seek help from a professional resumé writer? They are listed in the telephone directory and business section of the newspaper.

Sometimes help with resumés comes from unexpected sources. My friend was enrolled in a college course, and one of the things her teacher did was devote one week's classes to preparing a resumé.

Renee, a divorcee, had a similar windfall. While enrolled in a course on writing television commercials, she was assisted in composing a resumé. It was part of the curriculum, designed to help the students qualify for auditions. Renee wrote her resumé with the benefit of recommendations made by her instructor.

Money is not easily available to me. I was a homemaker before my divorce. Because I had no money to pay professional resumé writers, I wrote my own. Evidently I did well, because I landed a job in an insurance company as a clerical assistant.

Of course, it is possible to prepare a good resumé yourself. Libraries contain books to guide you. Talking about it with knowledgeable business friends is helpful. Refer to the resumé at the close of this chapter, and you will see it contains a constructive framework for your own history of experience. Most resumés indicate schooling, provide information about paid or volunteer work, and list personal interests, hobbies, awards, and anything unique about the individual's experience. Refer to the appropriate section of whatever business writing handbook you select for advice on how to compose a cover letter. Experts say the cover letter serves as an important advance guard for the resumé.

I could rack my brains from today till tomorrow and still not know my qualifications. I've done no outside work at all, paid or volunteer, but now that I'm my own sole support, I've got to get going making a living.

Contact the Displaced Homemaker Network, Inc., at 755 Eighth Street, N.W., Washington, D.C. 20001, about their program of assistance to individuals who have not worked in the labor force and who need paying jobs in their middle years. The national office will direct you to the nearest local center where, free of charge, you can receive job training, help with assertiveness, career counseling, and aid with money matters and health care. In short, you will receive help in becoming qualified to enter the work force.

Qualifying is not my problem. What troubles me is how I could possibly squeeze my long life into two sheets of paper. On top of that, to be interviewed by a young person who cannot understand the hardships divorce imposes, for example its burdens of alimony, is just too much to take.

You may be aware of your personal problems but a good interviewer is primarily concerned with your job aptitude. Learn to separate the emotional from the factual and concentrate on your work abilities rather than the age of the interviewer or the hardships of divorce. Redirect your energy to developing a descriptive resumé. Be selective in what you include in the resumé. In summarizing your life experiences, concentrate on your most valuable marketing skills and experience. For instance, if you excel in organizational or problem solving skills, stress those. Omit unnecessary details.

Preparing or updating your resumé prepares you for action. You are ready to apply as soon as a possible opportunity presents itself. When you learn of an interesting position, out comes your resumé and off it goes in the mail. Or it is immediately available to accompany you to any job interview. One way of coping with alimony problems is to ready yourself for better financial opportunities, and an up-to-date resumé is part of that preparation.

Even with a resumé I am proud of, I have difficulty applying. I often get a feeling the interviewer thinks I'm over the hill.

A skilled interviewer is capable of putting the job applicant at ease. That's half of the interview scene.

The other half is in your hands, and if you acquaint yourself with some interview basics, perhaps you can even enjoy it.

Here are some guidelines: Speak with directness and clarity. Try to be self-assured and composed. Stress your abilities. Listen attentively to the interviewer's questions. Allow the interviewer to see that your personal skills and qualifications relate to the job in consideration. For example, if you are applying for a sales position, it's important that you show you are articulate and persuasive. In any interview, stress your experience. Be realistic about salary expectations. Answer questions clearly and briefly. Remember to *ask* pertinent questions about job details.

Study these guidelines. You should be able to go into an interview thinking, "This is going to be a valuable expenditure of time."

After an interview, follow through with a brief thank-you note, restating your qualifications and adding any important points you did not state in the interview.

Knowing what you can bring to an interview and understanding the interview process will help give you a sense of self-assurance.

It's Your Business

I'm a widower, retired from an exhausting retail business, but I doubt I'll be able to remain idle very long. I'm not interested in weighty responsibilities again, but I can't see myself working for someone else. In a little while, I'd be telling them what to do. I guess when it's time to get going again, I'll muster up enough steam for a small personal business.

When you are ready to recharge your business battery, no doubt you will draw upon the personality traits the United States Small Business Administration cites as characteristic of successful business people. Those ten traits are initiative, a positive attitude, organizational ability, quick and accurate judgment, perseverance, responsibility, leadership ability, industry, sincerity, and a high level of energy. Many retirees establish a small business of their own to provide them income and a degree of responsibility. Look at the faces of some of the owners in the food shops of southern communities. They are the faces of mature adults. Note the shop hours. Some read, "Open weekdays, 8 to 2, and Saturday, 9 to 2. Closed Sundays." It's clear some retirees have discovered how to run a retirement business!

Hours are something to contend with. I know! Since my divorce, my retired years hang heavy, so I am looking into fields related to law, where my long experience as a real estate attorney can provide some income and much gratification.

It makes good sense to take skills you have developed and apply them to a related field. An attorney could open a small legal advisory office or a real estate sales office. An accountant could become a financial adviser to retirees. Frank, a widower, opened a small ground maintenance management business in Florida. For absent homeowners he utilized his management skills as a former pharmacy owner. Others have transferred artistic skills to running galleries and arts and crafts shops. A needlepoint expert could open a knit shop or needlecraft store. If you have made a thorough study of relocating to retirement areas, your new business could well be a housing consultation service. The possibilities are endless.

It is true that possibilities are endless. And so are the knocks sometimes. Since my wife died, everything has gone wrong. First my retail store folded because the owner of the building recalled his property. I opened a new store, and it failed. When I established a new business elsewhere, the economy and interest rates knocked me dead. Now I'm retired without intending to be retired. And here I am, a young, middle-aged man.

What you speak about are business realities, often beyond the individual's control, that influence success or failure.

Many middle-agers currently employed in full-time positions have a "later life business urge." So they put in spare time investigating the feasibility of becoming entrepreneurs. In addition to asking themselves what business they wish to go into, they realize they must get answers to the questions of location, capitalization, running expenses, necessary skills, and realistic goals. That's just to determine the feasibility of their dream. Many enroll in basic business courses. They seek advice from agencies mentioned previously. Yet with all of this, the wise entrepreneur is aware that going into business is always risky because outside factors can and do affect success or failure. (Remember, too, to seek professional advice about investing your money in others' business ventures.)

Renee, a divorcee, went into business in midlife and "lost her blouse" because she neglected to check out the state laws.

Before you put your future retirement dollars into a business of your own, see a lawyer. That way you can avoid any conflict with local, state, or federal regulations. Partnerships are especially vulnerable to legal problems that can leave you holding the sack.

Fortunately, my business is successful. But just when I was looking forward to the fun and freedom of retirement, my husband died, leaving me alone with a small manufacturing business. The work years seem endless now.

Small business owners must be aware of possible changes during middle age that they should be prepared to deal with. Stress caused by death is very difficult, particularly at a time when the business owner may be considering tapering off at work. Business owners dealing with this problem have to live through their grief and talk about their loss. They may be well advised to seek professional counseling.

I guess I'm fortunate in my financial affairs. After the death of my second husband, I purchased my father's business, paying for it in ten years. Now my grown sons have entered the business. When I have had enough, I can retire.

Many small business owners undergo stress when the time comes to pick a successor. Be fair to yourself and put yourself in the position where you will never have to sell on rush. The way to do this, is to plan in advance. Speak to your lawyer or accountant about the dollar value of your business. Ask about your chances of selling when you need to. Clearly, it's an advantage to have reliable, caring partners, so that when the time comes to hand over the reins, the transfer is a smooth one. But, if you do not, knowing how to sell your business is a definite advantage. Either way this is a liberating assurance to have.

I hope to liberate myself from doing what I have done for twenty years, working for a furniture contractor in a responsible administrative position. When I retire, I intend to become a semi-independent real estate salesperson. That will provide me a good balance of freedom and responsibility. That's my idea of my own small business.

Planning in your middle years can make the transition from one career to another easier. Reassessing your goals in life can ease the stress you might otherwise experience when you retire. You can, for example, use your time to take real estate courses for the necessary examination for licensing.

I'm not waiting for retirement. I made a major change in my middle years, moving from the hustle and bustle of the city to a work place that affords me a combination of city convenience with the quiet of the suburbs. Now I operate my commercial real estate practice serving city clients from an apartment outside the city. Since I have always been single, it was my decision alone to make.

Sometimes it is possible to combine the best of both worlds. Some people planning to go into business in later life find another type of compromise viable: buying a franchise wherein they combine owning a business with working for someone else. For insight into franchising, send for a copy of Franchise Opportunities Handbook, to the United States Department of Commerce, Industry and Trade Administration and Office of Minority Enterprise, Washington, D.C. 20402.

I would not want to make a dollar investment in a franchise at this stage of life. I am a man alone, and I expect to retire to a different location where I can use skills learned while working for a major corporation in a small free-lance business of my own.

Many things are possible if you plan ahead. Set your goals and take appropriate action to put your plans in motion. This is what Zachary learned to do when he became a free-lance writer for a small newspaper in the town he retired to. He transferred his writing and tax skills from the accounting firm where he had formerly been responsible for a monthly tax newsletter. He had used his middle years to prepare for the change, and so was able to move from one career to the other without great difficulty.

Suppose the changeover is disrupted by health or disability problems. Isn't this the stage of life where health problems multiply?

Fear of disability and concern about what to do if homebound are common among mature people, especially if they need added income in retirement. That is why resourcefulness and a positive attitude are essential.

You may not face this situation, but let's suppose you do. Enterprising homebound men and women can earn extra money in telephone sales, wake-up services, mailing services, and other income producers manageable from the home. By being aware of opportunities, utilizing skills you have, cultivating a positive attitude, and keeping yourself flexible, you can often cope even if illness or disability strikes. Theodore Herzl, the late Israeli leader, once remarked, "If you will it, it is no dream." If you will it, you will find the proper agency or source of information, such as local newspaper business opportunity advertisements, for employment possibilities whether in good health or disabled. It is always wise, however, to investigate the reliability of companies advertising work for homebound people. Get in touch with the Better Business Bureau for advice. Be especially wary of companies that ask for even a small investment and also of undertaking work for companies located in another state.

I feel a little more secure now and aware that I can add to income, if necessary, in my older years.

The opportunities are there. Draw upon all the resources you developed in younger years, add to them, take whatever actions appropriate, and you will surely be able to supplement income in later life. It is yours to create.

Should You Work for Others or for Yourself?
An Inventory to Help Guide the Way

If you were to choose your new career today, what would your choices be? List the first ideas that come to mind.

1. _____ 2. _____
3. _____ 4. _____

Rank them in order of preference: Label your first choice A, second B, third C, and the fourth D.

Do you have a hobby you would like to build into a new career? If so, is it listed among the choices above? If not, add it.

Do you prefer working for yourself or for someone else? Circle your choice.

Which skills do you consider important for career choice #1?

1. _____ 2. _____
3. _____ 4. _____

What skills can you apply from your present position? _____
_____

What skills do you need to acquire? _____

How will you do this and where? _____

What special skills/awareness/knowledge do you need for self-employment?
_____
_____

How will you acquire them? _____

What is the first step required to set your new career plans in motion? _____

What succeeding steps can you think of?

1. _____ 2. _____
3. _____ 4. _____

WORK IS JUST A FOUR-LETTER WORD

What is the target date for taking the first step? _____

For the succeeding steps? _____

What job market or business market are you aiming for? ___

How will you promote your business or yourself? _____

Name one measurement you will use to determine if your career plans are viable. _____

Over what period of time? _____

WORTH SOMETHING?
We need some imaginative stimulus, some not impossible ideal such as may shape vague hope, and transform it into effective desire, to carry us year after year, without disgust, through the routine-work which is so large a part of life.
—WALTER PATER

Could One of These Be Your Business in Retirement?

candle shop
cookie shop
motel
babysitting service
painting/decorating
boat rental
flowers
tax service
Stockbroker
fund raising
videotaping service
electronic games
job-lots liquidator
real estate

woodworking
shopping services
metalworking shop
gardening
bookkeeping
word processing
  service
gourmet cooking
  school
firewood dealer
collection agency
house sitting
card shop

property
  management
cabins
animal shelter
antiques
delivery service
typing service
accounting
catering service
free-lance writer
photo service
temporary-help
  agency
bartering club

ADD IDEAS OF YOUR OWN:
_____
_____
_____
_____

WORTH SOMETHING?
A perpetual holiday is a good working definition of hell.
—GEORGE BERNARD SHAW

Sample Resumé Form

NAME: _____
ADDRESS _____
CITY, STATE, AND ZIP _____
TELEPHONE (INCLUDE AREA CODE) _____

MAJOR WORK EXPERIENCE (List in reverse chronological order last three or four positions. If employment has been as a homemaker, state that.)

From	To	Job Title (Brief statement of duties)	Company Name, Address, Product or Service
____	__	_____	_____
____	__	_____	_____
____	__	_____	_____

ADDITIONAL WORK EXPERIENCE (List part-time jobs or free-lance work that describe your experience qualifications)

From	To	Job Title (Brief statement of duties)	Company Name, Address, Product or Service
____	__	_____	_____
____	__	_____	_____

EDUCATION

Degree or Diploma	School	Expertise or Special Skills
_____	_____	_____
_____	_____	_____

MISCELLANEOUS EDUCATION (Brush-up courses, home study, seminars, or courses in specialized skills such as bookkeeping, typing, word processing, or computer programming.)

_____

_____

ORGANIZATIONAL AFFILIATIONS, COMMUNITY SERVICE, PROFESSIONAL SERVICE (List most important ones and be certain to mention any achievements, awards, or service recognition.)

_____

_____

PERSONAL INFORMATION (Include major interests, marital status and number of dependents, if any. If you think it advantageous to supply references give names, addresses, and phone numbers, as well as positions, of two or three people you know.)

_____

_____

WORTH SOMETHING?
In order that people may be happy in their work, these three things are needed: They must be for it: They must not do too much of it: And they must have a sense of success in it.
—JOHN RUSKIN

7
Legal Lookouts

Are You Ready?

Two things I must face are that I am alone and there are fewer years ahead of me than behind. I don't like to use the word death. However, I do find myself worrying about whether my will is up to date. I also wonder if I have provided for myself adequately in the event I am incapacitated. It's a lot to think of and not particularly pleasant.

So many middle-agers, and some retirees as well, avoid making decisions and taking action in these areas, even though doing so will afford them peace of mind, freedom, and security in later life. The unpleasantness of drawing up or revising a will or facing the realities of possible illness is upsetting. Such feelings are understandable. Nevertheless, sound legal preparation is one of the keys to well-being and security in later years.

So, as long as we are facing problems, what legal matters besides drawing up a will should the midlife single put in order?

If you have any plans that involve property, a substantial sum of money, agreements with others, a place of residence, or significant change in your way of life, you would be wise to seek professional help. What you do in each of these areas will affect your rights, obligations, and responsibilities, as well as any liabilities you may incur under the law. The charts at the end of this chapter provide specific guidelines.

Am I legally ready for retirement? How can I answer that? Every day I hear of changes and of new issues that have now become a part of the single's legal province.

You mean issues such as the pension division that Cindy and Fred discussed when they decided to divorce. Those planning for retirement have always been encouraged to discuss pension problems with their attorney if unable to understand what the pension provided and how it protected them. But Cindy and Fred had a different pension problem. They had channeled large sums of income into Cindy's teacher retirement plan and had counted on using this money to live on later on. So this was an item they negotiated when they contemplated divorce. Since they had used Fred's income to live on during their marriage, they worked out an arrangement in the divorce agreement to divide the pension money Cindy would receive in retirement.

Something similar happened to my friend Marcia. Everything she owned was registered in her husband's name while they were married. If it hadn't been for her attorney, Marcia would now own nothing except the clothes on her back.

Most people maintain property under joint ownership in marriage. Many middle-agers have lived in marital arrangements where they were equal partners, with everything the couple owned in both names. But there are cases where the marriage did not include such an arrangement, and the woman had to engage a competent attorney in order to receive her share of the couple's assets. Such was the case with Yetta, who had trusted her husband implicitly and did not think twice about having their properties registered solely in his name. When their marriage ended, she owned nothing. Her lawyer had to fight tooth and nail for his client in order for Yetta to receive an equal division of their property.

It is as important for single people as for married couples to engage an attorney.

How right you are. For example, Frank, a widower, had no immediate family to leave his estate to. He decided to consult with an attorney in order to set up an estate plan so that his life assets would be distributed in accordance with his wishes. If he died intestate, that is, with no will, state law would determine how Frank's estate would be divided. The results could be contrary to his wishes. Also, the lack of a will almost always means delay and maximum costs in settling an estate. Frank selected a tax attorney who was also a certified public accountant, figuring that these qualifications would best serve his interests.

Lawyers, Lawyers, Lawyers

I've never needed a lawyer before. I wouldn't even know how to go about selecting one. In the past, when we had to engage the services of an attorney, my late husband did the choosing.

To wait for those critical times when you must have an attorney is disadvantageous. Scout about now while time is on your side. In all probability, you will need the services of an attorney to draw up your will or to help plan your estate. Inquire of friends whose legal judgment you trust. Contact the bar association or the lawyers' guild in your area. Look in local newspapers for legal clinics advertising their services for divorces, incorporations, real estate closings, and simple wills. Examine the Martindale-Hubbell directory at your library for suggestions about attorneys. Line up the names of qualified lawyers today.

How does discovering what my friends like help me with what I like? I consider myself an astute person, and I respect my own judgment. But, as with everything else, experience is the best teacher. My good fortune is that I have had but one encounter with an attorney in all the years of my single life.

Question any lawyer you refer to about his or her professional credentials. What schools did he or she attend? What professional associations does he or she belong to? Employers hiring you question you at length about your credentials. Since you will be hiring the attorney, do the same to ascertain all you can about his

Legal Lookouts

or her credentials. Then see if you feel a good rapport between your attorney and you. It is an operational plus to have an attorney who is supportive and reassuring. At the end of this chapter is a chart to guide you further in selecting an attorney.

But once I have made my selection, how do I determine if I can afford the lawyer's services?

That is an important consideration and one of the reasons many people fail to consult a lawyer. The fear that the cost will be too high is naturally of concern to people who have retired and are living on a reduced income. They must be judicious about expenditures.

There is no question that legal fees are expensive. However, compared to possible financial losses that can occur when a lawyer is not consulted, though necessary, the lawyers' fees can be cheap indeed.

One possible way to control expenses is to refer to the legal clinics. They advertise their fees and have standard rates for simple wills, divorces, real estate closings, and other items. In the main, lawyers' fees vary according to the area you live in, the type of legal work called for, and often, your ability to pay. If money is a severe problem, legal aid societies offer lawyers' services free, and lawyers' associations will sometimes give direction or assistance that can save you major consultation fees.

My income is cut in half because of the alimony I pay. I cannot dole out large sums to an attorney. I wouldn't go to a legal clinic. For me, that's too impersonal. Do I ques-

tion a private attorney's fee on the telephone or when we meet?

Either way is appropriate, but if you want to save yourself important time, inquire on the telephone. Lawyers usually are willing to state their professional fees on the phone. Feel free to shop around for an attorney whose rates you can afford. If the lawyer you are interested in is too expensive for your budget, ask for a recommendation of someone whose services you can afford. Enid did this when she was looking for an attorney to represent her. She contacted a top-notch lawyer whom she respected professionally, but whose fees were too steep. When she asked that he recommend someone whose fees she could afford, he gave her the name of an attorney whom Enid found suitable both professionally and economically.

Perhaps I won't find a legal clinic emotionally gratifying, but they have grown popular where I live. Realistically, if all I need is advice about a standard real estate closing, I don't need anyone to hold my hand. But I am concerned to get the best advice I can for my money.

It is perfectly suitable to inquire about a lawyer's qualifications, whether you engage the services of a legal clinic or a private attorney. As a matter of fact, because legal clinics advertise openly in newspapers, on television, and on the radio, they are very much in the public eye. Whether this guarantees the qualifications of the attorneys is something to consider. But remember, whether private or public, your relationship with your attorney is privileged and any information that passes between you is confidential. It cannot be disclosed in court or used against you without your permission.

Power of Attorney

I wouldn't say it's constantly on my mind, but I am concerned about who will help me if I become disabled. Husbands and wives have each other, but here I am single, after twenty years of marriage. Who'll be there for me if I am incapacitated?

In planning in midlife for retirement, the single should be concerned with appointing someone to represent his or her interests in the event of emergencies. One way to do this is to grant someone power of attorney, enabling that person to handle necessary legal affairs and to act in your behalf if you suffer an extended disability. Matters that can be managed by granting a power of attorney include everything from real estate transactions to writing checks to pay monthly bills.

Turn my life over to someone else? That's a wild one. I've been caring for myself all of my adult life. Why would anyone do a better job for me than me?

That is not the issue. If through misfortune you find yourself unable to act in your own behalf, either because of illness or accident, power of attorney, which you can grant to your lawyer or to anyone you choose, helps you to care for yourself. It can be drawn up to cover everything, that is, all of your interests, or it can be a limited power, authorizing someone to act on your behalf only in specific instances, such as paying your rent. To protect yourself, a general power, since it is very broad in scope, should be granted in special circumstances only. By the nature of the type of power of attorney you decide upon, general or specific, you keep control of the situation, since your representative can only execute what you have designated. What is essential is that you set yourself up adequately to handle emergencies, since you are alone, rather than waiting for when an emergency occurs.

Although after my husband died his estate left me fairly comfortable, there are nevertheless bills and expenditures that I find overwhelming. I never saw so much money go out. If I see a lawyer about a power of attorney, won't that be one more cost to me?

Yes, it will. Setting yourself up to handle your life effectively costs money. Sometimes not spending money to protect yourself is more expensive. Death is expensive for the survivor, both economically and psychologically. Where money is a problem, the person alone can execute her own power of attorney. A standard power of attorney form can be purchased in a commercial stationery store if you do not wish to have your attorney draw up an appropriate document. To assist you in determining what you should look for in granting power of attorney, refer to the "To Whom Should You Grant Power of Attorney" chart at the end of this chapter.

LEGAL LOOKOUTS 173

When a Letter Is a Helper

I recently learned about something called a Letter of Instruction. A divorced friend told me he wrote one so his grown children could carry out his wishes when he died. Can a letter do that?

Letters of Instruction do precisely that. They tell someone how you wish your personal affairs handled and should accompany your will and power of attorney. A Letter of Instruction does not have the legal impact of a will, but it is a wonderful helper for the person handling your personal matters. Refer to the chart at the end of the chapter for more about letters of instruction.

I can use all the help available. Tell me more.

Whereas a will deals with legal disposition of your effects after death, a Letter of Instruction elaborates on your personal affairs. For example, you can leave instructions about the handling of personal matters or designate the location of your income tax returns in your letter. While a grant of power of attorney enables a person you trust to act on your behalf during illness or absence, a Letter of Instruction tells a trustworthy person how actually to handle your affairs.

Sounds like an excellent tool for singles. What I do not have the opportunity to speak about, I can write.

That is the way to view it. A Letter of Instruction is an informative, viable way to execute your wishes upon death or if ill or incapacitated. The letter should be addressed to someone you trust and should be clearly written so that your instructions can be carried out with ease.

What do I do with it after it's drawn up?

One copy should be sent to your lawyer or executor and attached to your grant of power of attorney. Another should be clipped to your will. Still another should be located with your financial papers and other records. Some people keep a manila envelope or file of vital papers. That would be a good place to insert your letter of instruction.

I feel more protected already.

It is not so difficult, is it? When singles face up to situations, taking the time and spending the money for important legal protection, they can enjoy years of inner peace and bountiful living without further worry about things being taken care of in the event of crisis. Avoiding and postponing often ends in misery and sometimes, in the long run, results in additional expenditures. Surely you prefer the former to the latter.

Yes, You Have an Estate

Me? Have an estate? How preposterous! I've worked all my married life, and now that my marriage has failed, the law gave my ex-wife most of what I worked for and accumulated over a lifetime.

Everyone has an estate, whether it's just one piece of furniture in your home, only the clothing in your closet, or nothing more than the books on your shelves. Naturally, each person's estate varies in size depending upon what he or she accumulated over a lifetime. Some people have more, some less. Divorce may have reduced the size of your estate, but you still have an estate. It amounts to the total of all you own, plus all that others owe you, less all that you owe. That is your estate or net worth. It is something to think about. Maybe your estate is larger than you think.

My late husband protected me most of my adult life. He took care of money matters, of legalities, and of anything that would rock the boat. His wish was to save me from worrying about things I did not understand. But because of this, I am now going through much turmoil in learning to handle matters myself.

Now that you are at the helm, it is important you arrange for the proper management of your estate. Aim for securing your life now and in retirement. Experts in estate planning usually recommend that people who suddenly find themselves alone take an ultraconservative position, handling only those legal matters that must be dealt with immediately. Do not make radical changes and take the advice of trusted advisers only. Designating terms in your estate planning for your own medical care is important. Now that you are single, your own estate plan should be a priority because it will enable avoiding a tax bite upon your death. You can preserve capital to last you your lifetime through the establishment of trusts through money distributions. Or you can arrange to exhaust funds while alive, if that is your choice. Planning your estate with the aid of trusted advisers also keeps you informed of changes in the law that affect your estate.

I have been remiss in putting my estate in order. I should attend to it, particularly since I have accumulated some properties and a valuable art collection.

Good that you are ready to plan your estate. Decide first with whom you will consult. Will it be an attorney, a certified public accountant, a banker, a financial consultant, or a combination of two or more, depending upon the size of your estate? Next, think about whom to name as executor or executors. Is it to be a trusted friend, a relative, your lawyer, the trust department of a bank, or a combination of these?

When Jane was divorced, she was awarded a house and other assets, and she had to name an executor for her estate. While her estate was not very large, there was enough to consider avoiding taxes when she died. Jane named two executors—her brother, a physician, and her cousin, a businessman. Jane chose them because they could be trusted to carry out her wishes, caringly and astutely.

How astute must I be? When I exit from this world, the size of my estate will be the same as when I entered this world—zero! I'm divorced and planning to use my worldly assets for the pleasures of today's life, especially since I've had such unhappiness in my life. That

Legal Lookouts

means there's no estate planning for me to do.

Wrong! If you should die suddenly, before using up all of your estate, the government will tax what remains of your estate according to its net value, and the rates advance steeply by stages. Another consideration is that estate planning can develop a definite program for the prudent use of your assets during the remainder of your life, which is always important. Who can predict the future? Suppose you are ill and need funds to care for yourself? Planning your estate could provide for this and the healthy times to follow.

As we go on, it becomes more and more apparent that I should plan my estate. My late husband and I worked hard to accumulate what I now have. Should I be working up trusts and planning my estate so that upon my death, my children get more and the government less?

Estate planning is complex and the value of guidance by a knowledgeable attorney is that that provides your estate with the maximum protection from taxes.

A trust is an agreement under which all or part of your assets are held and managed by a trustee as specified for the benefit of your beneficiaries or yourself. Trusts come in many forms, and you can decide what is best for you. A trust can be used to conserve an estate and provide income for a surviving spouse or other beneficiaries. Or a trust can arrange for your property to serve your desired purpose after your death. Finally, you can arrange for a living trust to free you from the management of your estate and at the same time provide you a regular income.

There is no question that I want to leave my children a legacy when I die, and I intend to establish a trust if my lawyer concurs. Their life has been so hectic, what with the divorce and all, that I want them to remember me with love after I am gone.

Since the law changes from time to time, remember to see your lawyer about any trust you establish. Changes in the law could affect the legacy of your heirs. Furthermore, both the size of your estate and your purpose in planning its disposition influence the type of trust your lawyer will recommend. For example, the testamentary trust, which would become effective upon your death, provides that assets need not pass to heirs immediately and is not subject to inheritance taxes until they do. This type of trust could provide lifetime income for you, after which the remainder goes to your children or other heirs. The life insurance trust, another type you could establish, provides that the trust receives the policy's proceeds to meet the expenses of settling an estate, after which it provides for immediate income to heirs. As for living trusts, not only could this type of trust provide you with some retirement income, it also provides for the eventual distribution of the principal, while avoiding probate, in which the court oversees settlement of the estate. Discuss what type of trust suits you best with those involved in planning your estate with you.

Will my lawyer advise me if an administrator's fee on my estate will have to be paid out of estate funds?

Some executors, those who administer the estate, choose to waive the fee. This often occurs if close friends and family are named as executors. If an institution executes your estate, a fee is usual. Your attorney will be able to answer this question in more detail.

Where There's a Will

I've been told to see an attorney about writing my will. I've had my fill of attorneys what with my long-drawn-out separation and divorce. I wish I could muster up enough energy to write my will myself.

Never try to write your own will. It is far better to move quickly to have an attorney prepare a carefully planned will. This could make life much easier for your heirs, since lack of a sound will could create serious problems. For example, if you die with no will (intestate), distribution of your estate could go contrary to your wishes. Also, you can avoid maximum costs and delays in settling your estate that result when you have no will. If money is tight, engage the services of a legal clinic for a flat, inexpensive fee. Or seek advice from the Legal Aid Society about locating a lawyer whose fees you can afford.

But in which state should I draw up my will? Right now my home is in New York, but I may move to Arizona when I retire.

Right now, since you reside in New York and are subject to the laws of the state of New York, your attorney will construct your will to conform to New York's laws. If you move to another state, your will should be revised immediately to comply with the laws of that state.

There's something else that's important, and that is to rework or update your will so that changes in the law work for you. I have a superb accountant who sends me mailings about new laws, trends, and innovations. As a single woman, I find this very helpful.

Keeping up to date is extremely important. Make an effort to learn of changes in the law that affect disposition of your holdings, and be certain to question your lawyer about changes you need to make in your will. Sometimes, for example, you may wish to add heirs—when you become a grandparent. Other times, deaths mean the deletion of beneficiaries. If the nature of your estate has changed, or its size is altered, you should also change your will. Keep alert to changes in the law that could affect your will, such as new legislation governing estate and gift taxes and their exemption or exclusion features.

What about changes in the law affecting disposition of property? Many women who are alone are thinking of selling their house or buying a new one in another location.

You mention a very important fact. Changes in federal law may affect the capital gains tax on the sale of a house. That may depend upon your age and how the house was acquired by you. If you are considering the sale of the property, speak to your attorney.

Single women homeowners are becoming the fastest growing group in that market. One-third of the nation's condominiums and one-tenth of its houses, according to the National Association of Realtors, are being bought by women. Home ownership by women, whether always single, divorced, or widowed, and women's ability to borrow mortgage money has been made easier by federal laws passed in 1974 and 1975 that struck down sex discrimination in lending and home buying. Changes in social attitudes and the confidence the feminist movement gave women have also had an influence here. If property you own is to be included in your will, it is best to keep abreast of future changes in the law that could affect disposition or acquisition of property.

It's a New World Legally

I'm amazed how many things are different from when I grew up. I'm a widower, and if I decide to marry again, I would certainly execute a prenuptial agreement to be certain that my lifetime acquisitions go to my children. After all, they've been part of my life longer than any new wife. Furthermore, I want to leave them a legacy.

Stan, a widower, felt the same way. His opinion was that prenuptial agreements, though they may not appear romantic, are usually wise in a late or second marriage.

A prenuptial agreement is a contract between your prospective spouse and you, signed before and in contemplation of marriage. The agreement can strengthen a second marriage by clearly defining who owns what and where and how that shall be divided in any later disposition of assets.

It is interesting to note that more and more women are entering marriage with property, money, or interests of their own to protect. For them, a prenuptial agreement is a contract carefully negotiated by attorneys for two individuals with equal bargaining power.

I find this offensive. Even though I'm divorced, I'm still a romantic at heart. I think planning to share lives, but not possessions, could wreck a late marriage.

Herman, a widower, is a very romantic man. Yet when he met Elise, a divorcee, he spelled out his conditions very clearly. He proposed a relationship leading to marriage. He asked Elise to sign a prenuptial agreement renouncing any interest in his present estate. Though he vowed to support her handsomely, he intended to have his attorney clearly specify the financial and property rights of each spouse, defining what belonged to whom. The agreement would be backed up by carefully coordinated wills. Elise found this a reasonable arrangement.

It is not necessary to have large holdings to draw up a prenuptial arrangement. If marriage in midlife or older years involves the merger of existing families with entrenched spending habits and established wealth, the prenuptial agreement helps prevent conflict by clarifying precisely who owns what. It can also allay the concerns of children by previous marriages.

Legal Lookouts

I'm an old-fashioned man, troubled to read about unmarried couples of any age living together under formal agreements. Isn't it strange that the law would encourage middle-agers to play house?

There are people who view cohabitation agreements with good will and maintain that true love can survive some practical thinking. Then, there are others who think that cohabitation agreements bring a dollar coldness to romantic relationships. In New York State, there is a specific statute eliminating legal recognition of common law marriage, so cohabitation agreements must be expressed rather than implied. They are enforced just as prenuptial agreements are enforced. It is best to check your state's laws regarding cohabitation and prenuptial agreements, as these vary from state to state.

It's a new world for women, isn't it? As middle-aged women seek greater independence and freedom, they handle legal matters better. I'm particularly pleased with the way women who are alone are doing this.

Yes, they are rising to the challenge, learning about their rights and handling more of their lives on their own. A simple book to send for is "Your Rights Over Age 50", which can be ordered through the Circulation Department of the American Bar Association, 1155 East 60th Street, Chicago, Illinois 60637. It costs $1.00 and in forty-one pages presents questions and answers dealing with the legal rights of those between fifty and sixty-five. Another important booklet to send for is "A Woman's Guide to Social Security," available from your local Social Security office, or from the United States Department of Health and Human Services, Social Security Administration, Washington, D.C.

Let's not limit ourselves. Whether male or female, all single people should know their rights under Social Security.

Yes. Visit your local Social Security office and speak to a counselor. If this is not possible, send for free booklets on estimating your Social Security retirement check; how to earn Social Security credits; survivor's benefits; rights of the aged, blind, and disabled; and Medicare. Or you may wish to buy *The Complete Social Security Handbook* by Bryce Webster and Robert L. Perry. This is a detailed guide to Social Security, Medicare, and Medicaid.

Putting Legal Affairs in Order

List any situations involving legal obligations and possible risks in which you would be wise to have professional legal advice before proceeding. Start off with those indicated, then add your own.

1. Making or revising a will

2. Selling a house

3.

4.

5.

6.

7.

8.

9.

10.

11.

12.

LEGAL LOOKOUT:
The law is the last result of human wisdom acting upon human experience for the benefit of the public.
—SAMUEL JOHNSON

A Legal Checklist

Legal Considerations	Check if Completed	Dates You Will Attend to This
1. Making or revising a will		
2. Prenuptial agreement (if planning a late or second marriage)		
3. Power of attorney		
4. Letter of instruction		
5. Selling your home		
6. Mortgaging your home		
7. Buying a home or condominium		
8. Leasing a house or apartment		
9. Investing in land		
10. Setting up your estate plan		
11. Making substantial gifts to children		
12. Setting up a trust fund		
13. Establishing a new business		

14.	Planning a joint venture or partnership	
15.	Handling the affairs of an ill or incompetent relative	
16.	Lending or borrowing a sum of money	
17.		
18.		
19.		
20.		
21.		

LEGAL LOOKOUT:
Where laws end, tyranny begins.
—WILLIAM PITT

To Whom Should You Grant Power of Attorney?

- Naturally, it should be someone whose judgment you trust.
- Someone who is well-informed and knowledgeable.
- Someone open-minded and able to weigh matters objectively.
- Someone who cares about you and your interests.
- Someone confident enough to take the initiative on your behalf when the situation calls for it.
- Someone capable of handling responsibility.
- Someone who has excellent references from people you trust.

These may appear to be tall qualifications. But then again, single preretiree, your retirement legal matters deserve the best planning. What qualifications would you add?

-
-
-
-
-

LEGAL LOOKOUT:
Whene'er you speak, remember every cause Stands not on eloquence, but stands on laws.
—JOSEPH STORY

Legal Lookouts

Become an Aware Judge When You Select a Lawyer

Important questions to ask a lawyer you are interviewing are:

1. How long will it take to arrange my legal affairs?
2. What are your hourly and contingency fees?
3. Will you itemize your fees?
4. Are you available on the telephone to help me, too?
5. What kinds of legal matters have you specialized in?
6. When have you handled similar matters?
7. Why do you think you are the right person to handle my legal affairs?
8. Do you use the assistance of paralegals in your practice?

Add your own questions:

9.

10.

11.

12.

13.

> LEGAL LOOKOUT:
> A lawyer without history or literature is a mechanic, a mere working mason; if he possesses some knowledge of these, he may venture to call himself an architect.
> —SIR WALTER SCOTT

Letters of Instruction

Legal matters where letters of instruction are valuable:

1. Safe deposit box
2. Loans outstanding
3. Income tax returns
4. Investments
5. Social Security
6. Checking accounts
7. Personal effects
8.
9.
10.

LEGAL LOOKOUT:
Even when the laws have been written down, they ought not always to remain unaltered.

—ARISTOTLE

Example of a Portion of a Letter of Instruction

MEDICAL INSURANCE:

    Coverage: _____

    Company: _____

    Address: _____

    Policy number: _____

    Location of policy: _____

    Through employer or other group: _____

    Agent, if any: _____

    [Repeat for all insurance policies.]

Additional Examples of Letters of Instruction

1. CREDIT CARDS

   All credit cards in my name should be canceled or converted to your name.
   Company: _____ Phone: _____
   Address: _____
   Name on card: _____ Number: _____
   Location of card: _____
   Repeat for each card.

2. LOANS OUTSTANDING
   (OTHER THAN MORTGAGES)

   Bank: _____
   Address: _____
   Name on loan: _____
   Account number: _____
   Monthly payment: _____
   Location of papers: _____
                   (and payment book, if any)
   Collateral, if any: _____
   Life insurance on loan? ☐ (yes) ☐ (no)
   Repeat for all loans.

LEGAL LOOKOUTS

3. CAR

   Year, make and model: _____
   Body type: _____
   Cylinders: _____
   Color: _____
   Identification number: _____
   Location of papers: _____
                 (title, registration)
   Repeat for each car.

4. INCOME TAX RETURNS

   Location of all previous returns—federal, state, local:

   Our tax preparer: _____
               (name, address, phone)
   Check: Are estimated quarterly taxes due?

A List for Your Survivors*

Contemplating death, and the consequences for our survivors, is not a pleasant chore but it's an essential part of estate planning. It's also a compassionate act if it leads to eliminating some confusion and uncertainty for the person who is newly widowed.

CHECKLIST FOR THE SURVIVING SPOUSE

CPAs often advise estate-planning clients as one of their first actions to draw up an inventory of the documents a survivor will need, and also a list of people who can be turned to for help. In each case, they suggest, instructions should clearly indicate where a document is filed and where the adviser can be reached.

Key papers the survivor should be able to lay hands on at once begin with your will. (If you don't have a will, or the one you have is not up-to-date, it is most important that you have one prepared at once. In deciding how you wish to dispose of your assets, you will want to consult your CPA and other estate-planning advisers, including your attorney, who will actually draw up the will.)

Other documents the surviving spouse will need include

- [ ] Insurance policies. Not just the ones you took out yourself but also group policies provided by your company, policies issued in connection with the taking out of a mortgage or loan, National Service Life Insurance from your military days, or policies issued by fraternal or religious organizations.
- [ ] Pension plan papers, which usually provide for either final settlements or benefits for surviving spouses.
- [ ] Bankbooks, safe-deposit box records and keys, stock and bond certificates, evidence of real estate equities and other investment documents.

*Reprinted with permission of "CPA Client Bulletin" copyright © 1982, American Institute of Certified Public Accountants, Inc.

Legal Lookouts

- [ ] Ownership documents for houses, cars, boats and other major assets.
- [ ] Copies of mortgages; contracts for the performance of your professional services, especially if partially or wholly fulfilled; time payment agreements and other long-term commitments.
- [ ] Lists of debts owed to you and by you, including names, addresses and terms of the obligations.
- [ ] Records of charge accounts, credit cards, club memberships, etc., with suggestions as to which of these might be retained.
- [ ] Copies of income tax returns for recent years. These will be needed by your CPA-tax adviser, if he doesn't already have them, for preparing your final tax return as well as changing survivors' tax status.
- [ ] Birth certificate, marriage certificate, social security number, military discharge papers and other personal historical records.

Give Names, Addresses, Phone Numbers

Include on the list persons or organizations to turn to for advice or assistance:

- [ ] The lawyer who drew up your will.
- [ ] The executor of the will.
- [ ] Your insurance broker or agent. He also may be able to help in filing a claim for death benefits from the Social Security and Veterans Administration, including, perhaps, permission for burial in a national cemetery.
- [ ] Your stockbroker-investment counselor.
- [ ] Advisers in other investment areas, such as real estate, in which you may have been active.
- [ ] Your banker.
- [ ] The person at your company who arranges for payment of death or survivors' benefits.

☐ Your CPA-tax adviser.

ADD ITEMS OF PERSONAL ADVICE

Finally, write a note providing the sort of guidance or suggestions you can probably best supply:

☐ For example, if your securities were selected to meet your investment needs as a couple, will they still be appropriate for the single survivor whose needs are likely to be quite different?

☐ How should your business or professional practice interests be disposed of? This is something you might want to arrange yourself in advance, as with a buy-sell agreement with your partners, backed up by insurance that will provide the cash to liquidate your equity.

☐ Cash will be needed to meet current expenses until the estate is settled. Where can this be obtained?

LEGAL LOOKOUT:
Possession is eleven points in the law.
—COLLEY CIBBER

8
Putting It All Together

Have you met singles in their middle years or older, working or retired, who are basically happy?

There are men and women who appear comfortable with themselves. Unconcerned with perfection, these singles do not pressure themselves, but they are aware of goals for today and for later life. While alone, they are rarely lonely. Instead, their lives are enriched by exposure to people and interests, family and friends, careers and leisure. Inner growth is important to them, and their lives show direction and meaning. While these people have matured over the years, none of them arrived at a fundamental feeling of self-satisfaction in a day. They carefully planned and took action in order to achieve their goals. When they faltered, they picked themselves up—sometimes with the help of others—dusted themselves off, and started all over again. If, for example, a business venture soured, instead of quitting, they reentered the competition from a different position.

I've met mature singles like that. They don't dwell on trivia or negatives. Age seems to be secondary. And they always have interesting things to talk about. I like them because they are positive people.

People enjoy being with others who make things happen. People who have expanded their lives through careers, hobbies, or travel have interesting experiences to relate. They meet interesting people as a result of their endeavors. Since so much is happening in their lives, they are usually bursting with news. They do not have time for, nor are they interested in, gossip or complaining. Humor is part of their personality, yet never at the expense of others. Humility is evident, too, for they are aware of the struggle they went through to arrive at where they are and grateful to be successful. They accept themselves for their strengths and weaknesses. You rarely hear them defending themselves to others or behaving aggressively. They enjoy today and, at the same time, plan for tomorrow. When they retire, they retire from work, never from life.

Can you be more specific?

There are singles in midlife or older who are making the most of their present lives and loves.

A twice-widowed friend is risking marriage again with a man who has a heart condition, even though both her previous husbands died of heart attacks. Her new fiancé is there for her all the way—his condition is physical, not psychological. While Jennie is worried about his health, they are nevertheless planning a future in a nearby state.

Then, there is twice-divorced Emmanuel, who is teaching himself to live independently and concentrating on building his professional practice. He now chooses to live alone. In the past, he rushed into relationships because he did not have the courage to live alone. His philosophy today is that independence leads to greater interdependence because people have so many opportunities to develop their potentials.

Cynthia, a widow, is working out her survival with the help of a therapist. Her life has changed after thirty-four years of marriage, and she is fighting off depression. She is trying to add purpose and direction to her new life, not only to live today, but to feel alive into tomorrow.

Some singles are examining their present lives, making selective changes if they are not pleased. Leticia, for example, not only had the courage to end an unhappy marriage of twenty-three years, but to enter a new career.

There are singles who are exploring new avenues of adventure they never dared to try before. Henry, who has been divorced eight years, recently traveled for the first time, putting his leisure hours to exciting use.

Many singles cherish their ties to the younger generation. Anthony, a widower, has grandchildren who are precious to him and in whom he sees an extension of his own life. He has planned his small estate so that they will profit later, and he enriches his retired days by sharing his time with them now.

Margie, who has always been single, is sharing too, by working as a volunteer in a political organization. And Selma, who is separated from her elderly husband, is a regular visitor to her mother, who is in a nursing home.

Selma respects herself enough to give love to her aging parent, and this makes both of them feel even more worthwhile. Meyer, who is separated from his wife, has reorganized his health program, eating more sensibly and exercising more often because he prizes his own well-being. Bessie, a retired widow, purchased a time share near Tanglewood, Massachusetts, so that she could spend her two weeks vacation living elsewhere independently and enjoying fine music.

Carolyn, a widow, has developed new friendships with others who share the same values and interests. She put aside chronology, substituting intelligence, character, and personality. Her friends range in age from twenty to eighty, and Carolyn insists she has more than expanded her horizons.

There are singles like Enid, who was incapable of supervising her own finances but is doing it now.

All of these people feel good about growing and being in charge of their lives. Each of them is developing skills in midlife to extend into their retired years. When they retire, if they retire, they will see retirement as a beginning, rather than an ending. To them life is always a beginning, even when they end something.

Is that what you mean by putting it all together?

Exactly. It is you working for you. It is everything inside of you working together, the mind with the spirit, the social with the emotional, and the intuitive with the intellectual. It is using all of your resources and capabilities to make plans, set goals, and take appropriate action in leisure, housing, careers, health, legal affairs, and finances, to give yourself the best of everything now and into later life. Benjamin Franklin understood this. He said, "Doest thou love life? Then, do not squander time, for that is the stuff life is made of."